Jane S

IELTS Graduation

Teacher's Book

MACMILLAN

Macmillan Education
Between Towns Road, Oxford OX4 3PP
A division of Macmillan Publishers Limited
Companies and representatives throughout the world

ISBN: 978-1-4050-8079-8

First published 2007

Designed by eMC Design; www.emcdesign.org.uk
Cover design by Macmillan Education
Illustrated by eMC Design and Peter Cornwell

The authors and publishers would like to thank the following for permission to use copyright material:

Extracts from *Greenpeace online* www.greenpeace.org reprinted by permission of the publisher.

Extract "*Number working past retirement age set to double in 10 years*" by Sarah Womack © The Daily Telegraph 2005 reprinted by permission of the publisher.

The publishers would like to thank Frances Cook for all her hard work on this project.

Printed and bound in Spain by Edelvives

2011 2010 2009 2008 2007
10 9 8 7 6 5 4 3 2 1

Introduction

Increasing numbers of international students wishing to study at colleges and universities in Britain, Canada and Australasia need to achieve a high band score in IELTS in order to do this.

IELTS Graduation is designed to help students develop the academic language and exam skills necessary to achieve an IELTS band score of between 5.5 and 7.5. For students at a lower level than this, we recommend studying *IELTS Foundation* first.

The course consists of the following components:
Student's Book
Teacher's Book
Audio CDs
Study Skills Book (with Audio CD)

Coursebook

IELTS Graduation consists of 10 interesting topic-based units. Each unit contains comprehensive practice in Reading, Writing, Speaking and Listening with each part of the test broken down and explained, and exam skills practised. The units also contain Language Focus sections, which analyse the main grammatical areas relevant to a higher IELTS level, together with Vocabulary sections focused on common IELTS topics. There are also regular pronunciation sections as well as pages developing Study skills.

The back of the book contains further grammatical explanations and exercises along with extra vocabulary work. There are also complete model answers for all the Writing questions accompanied by useful comments. Complete scripts for all the Listening exercises are in the back of the book.

The contents are closely based on the IELTS exam assessment criteria and each of the 10 units integrates the four skills thus providing balance and variety. The book also aims to develop the type of skills necessary to study and perform effectively in an English-speaking academic environment and active learning is encouraged. Therefore, *IELTS Graduation* combines two key elements: IELTS preparation and essential study skills.

For a detailed description of each unit see Contents on pages 8 and 9.

Teacher's Book

The Teacher's Book provides the keys to exercises including line references indicating where answers to reading text questions can be found, clear teaching notes for the activities in the Student's Book and ideas for making the best use of the Student's Book material. For teachers with little experience of teaching IELTS students, the Teacher's Book gives detailed information about the IELTS exam and the strategies and techniques necessary to achieve a good band score.

In addition, it also offers insights into English for Academic Purposes (EAP) and the crucial role that study skills play. This information can be found in the Aims sections of the teacher's notes.

Recording scripts with highlighted answers are included as well as a number of suggestions for optional activities that can be used to supplement the core materials of the Student's Book.

There are 10 Photocopiable practice activities at the back of the Teacher's Book, related to each unit in the Student's Book. These activities reinforce work done in class. Detailed feedback and model answers can be found in the Key for this section.

Study Skills Book

The *Study Skills Book* can be used for self-study or as an intensive IELTS preparation course. It is divided into four sections to give further practice in the Listening, Speaking, Academic Reading and Writing modules of the IELTS exam. This workbook includes relevant exercises, sample answers and useful strategies on how to be successful in the IELTS exam. Keys and comments are given for all the activities in the book and a complete IELTS practice exam is included. The *Study Skills Book* can be used both to supplement *IELTS Graduation* or as a separate course.

Core skills areas

Reading

Texts are taken from a variety of sources including newspapers, magazines and academic journals and are intended to have a broad appeal to students from a range of backgrounds and cultures. Texts become more difficult as the course progresses. In the later units the aim is to provide students with texts which reflect both the more academic subject matter and linguistic level of difficulty which they might expect to find in the actual examination. These texts are intended to challenge higher level students and care should be taken that lower level students are not discouraged by them.

In each Reading skills section, the student is given guidance in both understanding the text and in learning to deal with the full range of IELTS question types. Skills such as skimming, scanning, finding topic sentences and guessing the meaning of new vocabulary from context are developed through a series of tasks and students are also given support and useful tips for tackling each type of question.

Writing

IELTS Graduation encourages students to work on existing writing skills to achieve a higher band score in the Writing module. Features include planning, paragraphing, useful language, style and editing. All units also contain an IELTS Writing question to give individual practice.

As well as focusing on the writing process, a product approach is adopted by basing tasks on model or authentic student writing. This gives insights into the type of text required and the level of the language that is desirable. These sample answers also develop students' ability to evaluate their own work more successfully. Relevant language is highlighted and tasks are often complemented by grammar or vocabulary exercises which also help improve students' writing. Model answers and comments can be found on pages 189–196 of the Student's Book.

Speaking

IELTS Graduation provides guidance and strategies on how to approach the Speaking module. There are numerous opportunities to practise all three parts of the module on a range of topics. Peer and teacher feedback, as well as self-evaluation, are drawn upon to help develop speaking skills. Recordings of authentic student responses are also used for activities and analysis.

To improve students' speaking skills in general, there are regular opportunities to speak in pairs, for example in pre- and post- reading and listening activities. In addition, language sections throughout the book provide useful words and phrases relating to particular functions such as giving and justifying opinions. Motivating tasks and interesting topics also allow students to present information and ideas or discuss key issues. These activities will be useful preparation for future academic contexts.

Listening

IELTS Graduation gives students practice in all four parts of the Listening module, as well as providing support and useful tips for tackling different question types. In addition, there are further listening activities designed to practise such skills as note completion and listening and writing simultaneously. This book also gives guidance on how to develop students' listening skills by focusing on key areas such as prediction.

Recording scripts are provided on pages 197–207 of the Student's Book and for easy reference are also given in the Teacher's Book notes where the answers to the questions are clearly marked.

Language focus

The Language focus sections have two main aims: to improve the level of accuracy by concentrating on those areas of language which commonly cause difficulty and to help students with those aspects of the language they need to be familiar with if they are to comprehend and produce academic language effectively.

The language work is integrated into the skills work, often highlighted in a reading or listening text. Students are this encouraged to notice language in context and to try to formulate the rules for themselves before going on to use the language in IELTS Speaking or Writing tasks. At this level, the emphasis is on the more formal language of writing and academic discourse.

Further practice of discrete language areas is provided in the Grammar section on pages 168–178 of the Student's Book

Vocabulary

The topic-based units help students to build up key vocabulary around such typical IELTS topics as the environment, health and crime. Students are also encouraged to increase the communicative quality of their speaking and writing by learning and using fixed lexical chunks. In addition, every unit contains a Dictionary focus section which highlights useful academic words contained within the unit, encouraging students to notice such language in context and to start to widen their own lexical range. Finally, the Vocabulary section on pages 179–185 of the Student's Book contains a range of extra activities, focusing on such areas as collocation.

Pronunciation

Pronunciation is a key component of the IELTS Speaking module and is an area that is often overlooked. *IELTS Graduation* contains regular pronunciation sections that cover a wide range of key issues such as final consonants, the schwa sound, connected speech and sentence stress. These activities are integrated into the units, allowing students opportunities for relevant practice.

Study skills

Each of the 10 units in *IELTS Graduation* has a Study skills section focusing on a particular area. The exercises enable students to develop more effective learning strategies. Students are encouraged to attain 'excellent learner' habits and to review and evaluate their work throughout the course.

The IELTS exam

IELTS, or the International English Language Testing System, is an exam designed to assess a learner's level of English, on a scale from 1–9 (see page 6 for details). A summary of each module is outlined below:

Listening

Content: This module is in four sections, which get progressively more difficult and takes about 40 minutes. The first two sections are based around social situations. Section 1 will be a conversation between two speakers, such as a conversation between a student and their landlord. Section 2 will be a monologue (one speaker) on a subject of general interest, such as a welcoming speech for new members of a sports club. The next two sections are more closely related to education or training contexts. Section 3 will be a conversation between two to four people, such as a seminar in which a group of students discuss a topic. Section 4 will be another monologue, such as a lecture, or a talk.

Question Types: There are forty questions in total, ten for each section. Different question types include multiple choice, completing notes or sentences, completing or labelling diagrams, charts or tables, classifying, matching and writing short answers.

Exam Tips: Each section is heard ONCE. However, there is time to look briefly at the questions before each part is played. During the exam, students should write on the question paper, and at the end of the exam have 10 minutes to transfer answers to the answer sheet. It is important they do this carefully, and check grammar and spelling, as mistakes will lose marks.

Academic reading

Content: The exam lasts one hour and there are three reading texts, of increasing difficulty, taken from newspapers, magazines, books and journals. The topics are of general interest, so students do not have to be experts in the subject area to understand them.

Question Types: There are forty questions in total. Question types include multiple choice, choosing *True/False/Not given*, or *Yes/No/Not given*; identifying the view of the writer; completing sentences or notes; completing or labelling diagrams, charts or tables; classifying; matching; choosing paragraph headings and writing short answers.

Exam Tips: As with the listening module, answers are written on an answer sheet, but no extra time is given for this. It is important for learners to practise managing time so that they complete the whole module within the hour by reading quickly and efficiently.

Academic writing

Content: There are two tasks in this module and it lasts one hour. In Task 1, students are expected to describe, compare and contrast information in diagrams, charts or tables using at least 150 words. This might be, for example, a chart showing how young people spend their leisure time. Organization is important and learners need to show that they can clearly present and describe data. Alternatively, students may have to describe the stages of a process, or explain how something works.

In Task 2, an opinion or a problem is stated and students need to write at least 250 words in response to a question related to this. They may be asked to give solutions to the problem, or present arguments in favour and against the opinion, as well as giving and justifying opinions.

Assessment: In Task 1, assessment is based on whether the question has been answered clearly and appropriately, the organization of the text and the accuracy and variety of vocabulary and sentence structure.

In Task 2, assessment uses slightly different criteria and is based on the arguments, ideas and evidence given, as well as the organization of the text and the accuracy and variety of vocabulary and sentence structure.

Exam Tips: Learners are advised to spend 20 minutes on Task 1 and 40 minutes on Task 2. It is important to keep to these timings, as Task 2 is longer, and carries slightly more weight than Task 1. It is also important to keep to the word limits, as writing less than the number of words stated is likely to result in a lower score.

Speaking

Content: The Speaking module takes between 11 and 14 minutes and is an oral interview between the student and an examiner. It will be recorded on audio tape. There are three parts to the module. In the first part, (4–5 minutes) the examiner will ask some general questions about home and family, job or studies, hobbies and so on. In the second part (3–4 minutes), the student is given a card with 3–4 prompt questions about a particular topic. They have one minute to prepare, when they can write notes if they wish, and will then be asked to speak on the topic for 1–2 minutes without any interruption. At the end of this section, the examiner may ask a question. Finally, in the third part (4–5 minutes), the examiner will ask some more questions related to the topic in the second part. In this section, they will be looking for the candidate to give opinions and express reasons.

Assessment: Assessment is based on fluency, the ability to express oneself clearly and naturally without long pauses, the range, variety and accuracy of vocabulary and grammatical structures, and pronunciation.

Exam Tips: It is important that the candidate tries to be as relaxed as possible in the exam. More extended responses to questions rather than just 'yes' or 'no' answers will gain higher grades. Students can prepare for this module, for example, by practising speaking for 1–2 minutes on different topics. However, discourage the memorization of long speeches as examiners can usually spot this, and will ask learners to talk about something else.

Band 9 – Expert User
Has fully operational command of the language: appropriate, accurate and fluent with complete understanding.

Band 8 – Very Good User
Has fully operational command of the language with only occasional unsystematic inaccuracies and inappropriacies. Misunderstandings may occur in unfamiliar situations. Handles complex detailed argumentation well.

Band 7 – Good User
Has operational command of the language, though with occasional inaccuracies, inappropriacies and misunderstandings in some situations. Generally handles complex language well and understands detailed reasoning.

Band 6 – Competent User
Has generally effective command of the language despite some inaccuracies, inappropriacies and misunderstandings. Can use and understand fairly complex language, particularly in familiar situations.

Band 5 – Modest User
Has partial command of the language, coping with overall meaning in most situations, though is likely to make many mistakes. Should be able to handle basic communication in own field.

Band 4 – Limited User
Basic competence is limited to familiar situations. Has frequent problems in understanding and expression. Is not able to use complex language.

Band 3 – Extremely Limited User
Conveys and understands only general meaning in very familiar situations. Frequent breakdowns in communication can occur.

Band 2 – Intermittent User
No real communication is possible except for the most basic information using isolated words or short formulae in familiar situations and to meet immediate needs. Has great difficulty in understanding spoken and written English.

Band 1 – Non User
Essentially has no ability to use the language beyond possibly a few isolated words.

Band 0 – Did not attempt the test
No assessable information provided.

Further information and strategies on how to approach the IELTS exam are detailed in this book, the Student's Book and the Study Skills Book.

Contents of the Teacher's Book

Contents of the Student's Book 8

1 Learn to succeed 10
2 Living together 18
3 Costing the earth 28
4 Healthy body, healthy mind 36
5 The world we live in 44
6 Going places 54
7 The world of work 64
8 Art and the city 72
9 Tomorrow's world 82
10 From me to you 91

Grammar key 101
Vocabulary key 103
Photocopiable exercises 105
Key to photocopiable exercises 121

Contents of the Student's Book

Unit and topic	Reading skills	Listening skills	Speaking skills	Writing skills	Language focus and Vocabulary	Study skills
1 Learn to succeed	Skim and scan reading Matching: headings to sections, opinions and people Sentence completion (from a list)	**Section 1** Form completion Map completion Table and diagram completion	Overview of the 3 parts of the Speaking Test	**Task 1** Changes over time Introductory sentences, describing trends, paragraph plan	Unreal sentence subjects (There is / was) Synonyms and parallel expressions Word formation: prefixes	Basic study skills and learning styles
2 Living together	Summary completion (from a list) True, False, Not Given	**Section 2** Note completion; Matching **Section 3** Multiple choice Table completion	**Part 2** Making notes	**Task 2** Understanding the question Argument / opinion questions: The balanced argument approach Linking general review	Sentence subjects Social issues vocabulary Word formation: nouns and verbs	Using a dictionary
3 Costing the earth	Multiple-choice, Matching Dealing with unknown vocabulary	**Section 3** Multiple choice, Summary completion	Pronunciation Final consonants **Part 3** Introducing and organizing your opinions	**Task 1** Selecting significant information Writing introductions Fixed time diagrams Making comparisons	Compound adjectives used in place of relative clauses Collocations	Recording vocabulary for Writing Task 1
4 Healthy body, healthy mind	Using headings to identify purpose and organization Completing tables, diagrams, notes Short answer questions Following and argument in a passage Multiple-choice questions:multiple answers Yes,No, Not Given	**Section 4** Multiple choice Summary completion	**Part 2** **Part 3** Food related topics	Essay sections Paragraph structure:The body of the essay Task 2 planning: finding ideas Argument / opinion questions: The opinion essay Describing opinions	Defining and non-defining relative clauses Participle clauses: -ing and -ed Medical terms vocabulary	Planning: Finding ideas
5 The world we live in	Matching headings (to paragraphs) Summary completion (no list) Labelling a diagram	**Section 2** Flow charts Short answers **Section 4** Short answer type questions Matching	**Parts 1, 2 and 3** Animal topics Expanding Pronunciation The schwa sound	**Task 1** Process diagrams Ordering, purpose and result.	The passive Adjectives and nouns	Academic vocabulary
6 Going places	Recognizing opinions in a passage Multiple-choice questions Completing a map Sentence completion (no list) Matching: People and opinions Understanding reference and substitution	Select the diagram **Section 1** **Section 4** Table completion	Making predictions **Part 2** Making questions **Part 3** Building speed	**Task 2** Understanding introductions Paraphrasing the question Writing introductions Introductory phrases Problem and solution questions Avoiding absolute statements	Lexical cohesion Conditional sentences	Editing your writing

Unit and topic	Reading skills	Listening skills	Speaking skills	Writing skills	Language focus and Vocabulary	Study skills
7 The world of work	Prediction True, False, Not Given Flow chart completion Matching information and sections Short answer questions Note completion Yes, No, Not Given Matching details to paragraphs	**Section 2** Prediction Short answer questions Sentence completion Table completion	Predicting the future Expressing certainty Pronunciation Connected speech	**Task 1** Multiple diagrams Ways of describing data Determiners	that-clauses Synonyms for people	Editing your writing
8 Art and the city	Distinguishing fact and opinion Matching:People and descriptions Summary completion (No list) Sentence completion (From a list)	**Section 3** Analysing multiple-choice options Short answer questions Note completion **Section 4** Discourse markers Multiple choice Sentence completion Short answer questions	Structuring what you say	**Task 2** Review: Balanced argument and opinion essays Refuting opposing arguments Giving and refuting opinions Writing conclusions	Linking expressions Types of buildings, furniture vocabulary	Improving your spelling
9 Tomorrow's world	Identifying the writer's purpose Yes, No, Not Given Matching: identification of arguments	**Section 2** Listening for dates and numbers Sentence completion Note completion **Section 4** Prediction Summary completion Diagram completion	Expressing likes and dislikes Pronunciation Sentence stress: Weak forms	**Task 1** Describing illustrations Maps	Academic vocabulary Expressing the future:probability Prefixes	Understanding question task words
10 From me to you	Identification of main idea and supporting information Multiple-choice questions Summary completion (from a list) Sentence completion Yes, No, Not Given	**Section 1** Multiple-choice: Diagrams Sentence completion Multiple choice **Section 3** Multiple options Table completion Summary completion	**Parts 1,2 and 3**	**Task 2** Keeping your focus Different question tasks Expecting the unexpected Stating your view	Articles Media vocabulary	Idiomatic expressions

1 Learn to succeed

Content overview

Themes

Unit 1 introduces the themes of education and gender. Students will read about issues related to gender differences in education throughout the world, and will be able to call on their own experience to discuss and compare approaches in their own countries.

Listening
- a dialogue about some of the problems international students face when they first arrive at university in England
- a description of a university campus in the UK

Reading
- gender differences in maths and science education

Writing
- interpreting diagrams and graphs
- paragraph planning for Writing Task 1

Exam related activities

Listening

Section 1 Form completion
Following directions on a map
Section 2 Short answers

Reading

Multiple choice
Sentence completion
Matching (headings to paragraph content, opinions and people)

Writing

Task 1 Describing changes over time in a diagram
Paragraph planning

Speaking

Part 2 Describing a course of study
Describing a teacher
Part 3 Discussing and comparing developments in education

Language development

Language focus

Verb tenses
Unreal sentence subjects: *there is/are, there was/were*

Vocabulary

Synonyms and parallel expressions
Word formation: prefixes
Describing trends

Skills development

Reading

Prediction of content
Skimming for gist (main idea)
Scanning for opinions

Writing

Paraphrasing
Organizing and writing essays
Revising and editing your writing

Listening

Listening for detail
Following directions

Study skills

Time management
Note-taking
Reading for key information

Dictionary focus

Building a vocabulary bank

Warm up p8

Ask students to look at the photos and elicit vocabulary related to educational subjects, teaching methods and gender preferences in education. Vocabulary may include: *single sex, mixed, sciences, arts, humanities, technical, vocational, future career, ability, skill, training, instruction.*

Reading p9

Skim and scan reading

Aim
The ability to skim and scan academic texts is an essential skill for university studies. As it is never possible to read all the books on a reading list, students must learn to read quickly for gist and select the texts that are relevant to their research or essay titles. The three reading techniques of prediction, skimming and scanning increase reading speed and allow students to read tactically, giving them time to focus on the most relevant sections of the texts.

Elicit predictions from the title of the article about the content and write them on the board. Include all predictions, however unusual. Students will be able to see which predictions are correct or incorrect when they have read and discussed the passage in detail (Exercise 2).

1 Ask students to read the title of the passage and answer questions 1 and 2.

Answers

1 C
2 D

2 Students skim the passage individually and compare the content with the predictions on the board in a class discussion. This is an opportunity to explain why some predictions may have been wrong. For example, students may not have paid enough attention to or may have misunderstood the keywords in the title.

3 Explain that when scanning for names and numbers we can limit our reading to looking for capital letters, figures and symbols.

Ask students to underline the keywords in each question. Go through the answers with the class.

Keywords: 3 year / OECD 4 average 5 professor / Yale 6 university / Dr. Elizabeth Spelke

Students scan the passage for specific information to answer questions 3–6.

Ask students to compare their answers with a partner and discuss any differences.

Answers

3 2003
4 10%
5 C. Megan Urry
6 Harvard

Matching: Headings to sections

Aim
Matching headings to sections is a way of testing that the reader understands the main ideas in a passage. As the heading in the question and the original passage will not have the same wording, it is important for students to look for synonyms (single words which have similar meanings) and parallel expressions (phrases that have similar meanings).

4 Students look for synonyms or parallel expressions for *controversy* (*fierce reaction*) and *inborn* (*innate*) in Section A of the passage.

5 Students match the sections of the reading passage to the headings to answer questions 1–5. Go through the answers with the class.

Answers

1 Section B ii
2 Section C v
3 Section D ix
4 Section E vi
5 Section F i

Matching: Opinions and people

Aim
In the IELTS Reading module, students will be asked to attribute opinions to people mentioned in the passage. This exercise gives students practice in scanning for names and finding the corresponding opinion.

6 First ask students to highlight the keywords in questions 6–11.

Keywords: 6 ability / brain / anatomy 7 attitude / performance 8 / 9 men / women / respect 10 / 11 ability / gender

After finding the opinions expressed in the passage, students should scan the passage again to link the opinions with the names of the people (A–G). Students work in pairs to answer questions 6–11.

Answers

6 C
7 E
8/9 D/F
10/11 B/G

Sentence completion (from a list)

Aim
Some of the expressions that answer the reading questions in the IELTS examination will be identical to those in the passage, but sometimes students will need to find parallel or similar expressions.

7 Refer students to the underlined words in questions 12–16 and ask them to highlight the parallel expressions in the passage. The questions follow the order of the passage. Parallel expressions are:

Question	Passage
12 learning capacity	aptitude (line 67)
13 language	verbal (line 70)
14 got better results in math	scored higher (line 93)
15 worst opinion	more negative attitudes (line 102)
16 effort	work harder (line 114)

Students complete questions 12–16 individually and check their answers with a partner.

Answers

12 F
13 C
14 E
15 B
16 D

Vocabulary p12

Synonyms and parallel expressions

1 Students work individually to match the expressions from the reading passage with parallel expressions. Students check their answers with a partner or the whole class.

Answers

1 c
2 g
3 h
4 i
5 d
6 f
7 a
8 b

Further practice

Refer students to Unit 1 Vocabulary, Exercises 1 and 2, page 179. If necessary, briefly revise the functions of nouns and adjectives.

Refer students to Photocopiable 1, Exercises 2 and 3 (TB page 106).

Students use parallel expressions to summarize the reading passage and discuss their answers. Point out that they should only write one sentence about the main idea of each paragraph and that they should not copy from the passage.

Word formation: Prefixes

Aim
As it is very unlikely that students will know all the words in a reading passage, it can be valuable for them to learn the technique of guessing the meanings of words from prefixes. Being able to identify the meanings of prefixes can help students develop both reading skills and vocabulary.

1 Elicit possible paraphrases of *neuroscientist* and *subcategory* as used in the passage. Elicit other associated words. Other possibilities are: *neurotic, neurosurgeon, neuron*. If students suggest *substandard, submarine* or *subscription,* you could explain that *sub* commonly means *under*.

2 Students can complete this matching exercise individually or in pairs. Disagreements can be discussed in a plenary session.

Answers

1 g
2 h
3 n
4 a
5 b
6 d
7 c
8 e
9 f
10 i
11 j
12 m
13 l
14 k

3 Students can do this completion exercise individually and compare their answers in pairs.

Answers

1 profit
2 final
3 write
4 graduate
5 president
6 information
7 annual
8 esteem
9 ability

Refer students to Photocopiable 1, Exercise 1 (TB page 106) to practise generating new words from prefixes.

Language focus p14

Unreal sentence subjects There is/was ...

Aim
Impersonal sentence subjects are used in scientific and academic writing to emphasize objectivity. The following exercises clarify and practise the use of these structures.

Explain that the normal word order in English sentences is subject/verb/object. However, in sentences beginning with *there is/was*, the grammatical subject (*there*) comes first and the real subject comes after the verb *(is/was)*. For example:

***There was a similarity** between male and female task performance figures in children under the age of 8.*

There	***was***	***a similarity ...***
(grammatical subject)	(verb)	(real subject)

In other words: ***A similarity existed** between male and female task performance figures in children under 8.*

Further practice

For a more detailed explanation of this structure, refer students to Unit 1 Grammar, page 169.

1 Students complete the exercise individually and compare their answers with a partner.

Answers

1 are
2 is
3 was
a singular
b plural

2 Remind students that the tense of the verb *to be* will correlate with the tense of the other verbs in the sentence. For example:

*... there **have been** scientists who **have suggested** ...* (both verbs in the present perfect)

Students complete the exercise individually and compare their answers with a partner.

Answers

1 have been
2 is
3 were
4 was
5 will ... be

3

Aim
The purpose of Exercise 3 is to raise awareness of word order. Students may have a tendency to put the participle after the verb *to be* as they would when forming a continuous or passive form.

However, in sentences beginning with *there + be*, the noun complement cannot be separated from the verb *to be*.

Explain that the verb and the real subject are not separated when the verb *to be* is followed by a present or past participle (*-ing or -ed*).

Further practice

Review the forms of the verb *to be* referring to Form in Unit 1 Grammar, page 168.

Ask students to work in pairs to find the correct form for each of the sentences in the reading passage.

Answers

1 b
2 a

4 Students rewrite the sentences using *There + to be ...* and the correct word order.

Answers

1 There was something unusual about the test results.
2 There was a loud noise outside the classroom.
3 There's no reason to believe that men are more capable than women.
4 There's someone waiting to meet you.
5 There were similar results obtained by Japanese boys and girls.

For further practice, write these prompts on the board and ask students put them in the correct order.

1 There / some healthy meals / being / are / sold / in school canteens.
2 There / healthy food / in some but not all schools / is / offered.

Answers

1 There are some healthy meals being sold in school canteens.
2 There is healthy food offered in some but not all schools.

Listening p15

Section 1 Form completion

Aim
In the first few days at university, students have to answer a variety of questions about themselves and may have to fill in a number of forms. The dialogues in the Listening section of this unit are typical of conversations with tutors taking students' personal details and giving general orientation.

Explain the different types of accommodation available to students in the UK:
university residence – purpose built accommodation on campus for the exclusive use of students during term time
host family – a family that takes international students into their home for a fee
shared house/flat – a rented house or flat which is shared by several people
bed-sit – a room which is both a bedroom and a sitting room / study

Explain the different types of answers required in this section. In this unit there are short answers (questions 1–6) and map completion exercises (questions 7–12).

Explain that for questions 1–6 (Exercises 1 and 2), students must limit their answers to **one** word.

1 and 2 1.1 Give students time to read the instructions and the questions, and underline the keywords (1 year 2 feeling 3 name 4 room 5 nationality 6 number).

Play the recording and ask students to answer questions 1–6 only.

Students compare their answers in pairs and discuss any differences. (The correct answers are underlined in the recording script below.)

Answers

1 first
2 confused
3 Sondra Da Costa
4 13
5 Spanish
6 07764 543302

1.1

[T = Tutor; S = Student]

T: Good morning, and how can I help you?

S: Good morning, my name is Sondra da Costa. I'm a first year student and I'm a bit confused about a few things. I was told by a lecturer to come here.

T: OK then, take a seat Sondra and let me see how I can help you. Because this is your first year here, I'll need a few personal details. What did you say your name was again?

S: Sondra da Costa.

T Is that Sandra?

S: No, it's spelt with an 'O'.

T: So that's S-O-N-D-R-A. And can you spell your surname, please?

S: It's D-A C-O-S-T-A.

T: Is that all one word?

S: No, it's two words, actually.

T: Fine, and are you living on campus or in other accommodation?

S: I'm living in university residences in Bramble House, the one on the main campus, room number 13.

T: How are you finding it so far?

S: Much better than I expected. I have quite a large room and we have a shared kitchen and bathroom. The other students I've met seem really friendly.

T: That's good to hear. I think you've made a wise decision living on campus. Now just a few more details and then we can go on to discuss what's worrying you. Where are you from?

S: My mother is from South America, but I was born in the north of Spain.

T: That's interesting and ... er ... one more thing ... Do you have a number we can contact you on in emergencies?

S: Yes. I have a mobile number. It's 07764 543302.

T: Let's just check that. Did you say 07764 543332?

S: No, it's 54-33-02.

T: That's fine, Sondra. Thank you. That's all the information I need for the moment.

Map completion

3 Revise vocabulary for places and locations from the Useful language box by asking students to answer 1–3.

Answers

1 next to Chemistry Lab A
2 Lecture Hall B
3 Go to the top of University Lane and turn left into Newton Drive. Take the first left and turn into Isaacs Street. At the bottom of Isaacs Street on the left is Lecture Hall A.

4 1.2 Explain that in this exercise students have to answer questions by listening to a conversation and following directions on a map.

On this recording, the tutor is explaining to the student how to find the Computer Rooms (in the Arts Block opposite Dalton House), the Library (to the right of Lab B), the Finance Office (at the end of Newton Drive), Students' Union (behind the cafeteria) and the Bank (in Isaacs Street, opposite Lecture Halls A and B, in the middle).

Play the recording for students to answer questions 7–12. The correct answers are underlined in the recording script.

Answers

7 G
8 B
9 C
10 E
11 F
12 (tutor not available all day) D

In pairs, students practise giving each other instructions to get from one building to another on the map.

1.2

[T = Tutor; S = Student]

T: So, how can I help you?

S: Well, I'm really worried about how I'm going to cope with university life ... I mean I feel like I don't know what's going on.

T: Don't worry, Sondra. Most undergraduates feel like this in their first week.

S: Well, maybe if I knew the campus a bit better, that might help.

T: Do you have a map of the campus?

S: Yes. I was given one during orientation week, but to be honest, I don't really understand it.

T: Well, let's look at it together. OK, we are here now in Dalton House. Opposite this building is the Arts Block where you'll find the computers. The Computer Rooms **(E)** are open from 9.00 a.m. till 10.30 p.m. weekdays, but closed on the weekends.

S: Are there no other computers on campus?

T: There are a few in the Library that are available throughout the year, except Sundays. To get to the Library **(F)** you keep going down University Lane, past the Science Block on your left. Opposite the Science Block are the Chemistry Labs and the Library is just on the right next to Lab B.

S: Fine.

T: Another important building is the Students' Union **(G)**. Turn left into Newton Drive. There are some trees and a little outside cafeteria. The Students' Union is just behind this.

One thing I must check ... have you sorted out your fees yet?

S: Well, I filled in a direct debit form so I suppose that means everything is fine.

T: Probably, but you should go to the Finance Office **(B)** just to make sure. It's at the end of Newton Drive. You'll need some identification ... your passport or student ID.

S: And is there a Bank **(C)** on campus?

T: Yes, it's open normal banking hours and there is a 24-hour cash machine. The Bank's in Isaacs Street which runs parallel to University Lane where we are now. Go past Lecture Hall B and the Bank is opposite, just before you get to Lecture Hall A.

S: Great.

T: Probably the best thing to do is to walk around and familiarize yourself with everything. Don't worry, it won't take you long to settle in.

S: I'm sure you're right. I feel a lot better.

T: I also need you to fill in this form for the tutorial file. Take it away with you and then make an appointment to see me again and we'll go over it. My telephone number is on the form, here, at bottom of the page. You can ring me anytime between 9.00 a.m. and 3.30 p.m. from Monday to Friday ... er ... except on a Thursday when I'm only available in the morning.

Review the answers with the whole class. Play the entire recording a second time to give students a chance to listen again and confirm the correct answers.

Note: In the IELTS Listening module, the recording is only played once. If you want to focus on exam practice rather than listening practice, only play the recording once.

Speaking p16

Understanding the test

Aim

In the Speaking module of the IELTS exam, students are expected to progress from describing personal experiences in informal language to adopting a more formal register to discuss and speculate on topics of global interest.

1 In pairs, students ask each other the questions and discuss their opinions. They then join another pair and compare their opinions in a group.

2

Aim

By making notes before the 1–2 minute talk in Part 2 of the Speaking module, students can organize their ideas logically. This exercise shows students the advantages of making clear notes in advance of the talk.

Point out that the IELTS topic card is a useful guide to developing the main points of the talk.

In pairs, students take one minute to make notes on topics A and B. They then exchange their notes with their partner and give a talk from each other's notes.

3 Ask students to underline the keywords in the questions.
1 future / teachers / smaller / role / education / students / Internet
2 compare single sex education / co-educational environments
3 physics / chemistry / more important / art / music
4 agree or disagree / learn / outside / inside classroom
5 differences / approaches / men / women / learning

Write questions 1–5 on slips of paper. In pairs, students pick a slip of paper at random and brainstorm the topic together. They discuss how to develop their ideas by answering the questions *Why ...?* and *How ...?* and by thinking of examples to illustrate their points.

Individually, students pick another slip of paper and prepare to discuss their topic with a small group.

Writing 1 p17

Task 1

1 Ask students if they can remember the answers to 1–5. Refer students to the front of the book. Students discuss any doubts in groups. Any unresolved questions can be clarified in a whole group session.

Answers

1 20 minutes. Use the time to select the most important data and identifying trends, organize your ideas. Write and edit your essay. Check you have an overview at the beginning and a conclusion at the end.
You should write a factual description of a diagram.
2 150 words in 2/3 paragraphs
3 Achievement, Coherence and Cohesion, Lexical Resource, Grammatical Range and Accuracy
4 No. You are only expected to describe the most significant facts. You are not asked for your opinion.
5 No. You should only include the most important data and the main trends.

2 In groups, students produce drawings A–H and label the diagrams with the words in 2. Each group draws one of their labelled examples on the board for whole class revision.

Task 1: Changes over time

3

1 Explain that diagrams may show changes over a period of time or compare several situations at a given moment, or both. By first establishing the time period, students will be able to decide which tense(s) they need to use in their Task 1 writing question.

Answers

Diagram 1: both
Diagram 2: comparisons only
Diagram 3: both
Diagram 4: comparisons only

2 Students review the forms of the tenses by completing Unit 1 Grammar, Exercises 1 and 2, page 169. Refer to the Tense revision section on page 168 to troubleshoot errors. Students work in small groups to discuss the tenses they should use to describe the diagrams.

Answers

1 past
2 present
3 past
4 future

3 When students have written the introductory sentences individually, they compare and discuss them with a partner.

4 Working in pairs, students draw diagrams comparing commercial or social trends in their country. Using vocabulary from the Useful language box, students write a description of their partner's diagram. Forming a group with another pair, students can
a) rephrase another student's description and/or
b) recreate a diagram from a description.

Students work in pairs to select suitable vocabulary from the Useful language box and extend the descriptions of Diagrams 1 and 3. After completing the descriptions individually, students compare and discuss their answers with their partner.

5 Before asking students to write descriptions of the main changes in the diagrams, review the type of information required (changes over time/comparison) and the tense *to be* used (past).

It may be helpful for students to discuss 2 and 3 before writing individual descriptions of the diagrams in 1.

Answers

2 a3 b1, 2 c4
3 For graphs, use a pencil to draw a line joining the first and last points. This will reveal the overall trend and make it easier to see if there are any major variations from that trend. For bar charts, use a pencil to connect the tops of the bars to see the main pattern. For tables and pie charts, circle maximum and minimum figures.

6 Brainstorm the answers to 1–6 as a whole class before asking students to work in pairs for Exercise 7.

Answers

1 yes
2 formal
3 past tenses
4 both
5 Student enrolment from three countries at one university in a five-year period
6 See model answer in Exercise 8.

7

Answers

- uses an informal register
- lacks precision
- *blue line* is meaningless
- errors with adjectives and adverbs
- inappropriate to give explanation

Students can refer back to the questions in Exercise 6 to establish the following:
- no dates and figures
- use of informal language (*Well, first of all, After a bit more*)
- use of wrong tense (past dates indicate past tense needed)
- no comparison between national groups
- no identification of groups or lines
- main features not highlighted
- unsupported opinion (*the strong Chinese economy*)

8 Check and discuss answers to paragraph 2 with the whole group. Encourage students to recognize that there is a range of possible correct answers.

Answers

1 enrolment of students, Japanese admissions, Chinese numbers, numbers of Indian students
2 almost, from over, just over, around, about, approximately
3 (*accept any suitable answers*) 1 grew steadily 2 sharp rise 3 in 2003 4 steady growth 5 decreased dramatically 6 a high 7 levelled off 8 from 2001 to 2002
4 The answer does follow the paragraph plan (page 20).

9 Before students answer 1–3, ask them to look at the diagram and identify:
- the percentage range (10%–40%)
- the time span (2003–2006 / 3 years)
- the starting point of each company (D 20%, C 25%, A 27%, B 28%)
- the finishing point of each company (D 35%, C 36%, A 27%, B 28%)
- the peak (36%) and the lowest point (17%) and the year of each (2004)

In pairs, students answer 1–3.

Answers

1 percentages
2 A changes little. B, C and D have all increased but by very different amounts.
3 See model answer on page 189.

10 Students write their answers for homework. In the next class, students work in pairs. They exchange answers, compare their partner's work with the model answer on page 189 and discuss differences.

Study skills p23

Aim
Students who can describe their strengths and weaknesses in each of the study skills will be in a better position to develop strategies for improving in problem areas.

1 Students complete the table.

Answers

Making notes during lectures: Paolo
Selecting key information when reading: Yuan
Learning new vocabulary: Yuan
Time organization: Paolo

2 and 3 Ask students to discuss individual study skills with a partner to decide their degree of confidence. Pairs can join together to form small groups and share strategies for developing study skills. Ask each group to present its strategies to the rest of the class.

Dictionary focus p23

Aim
As students' writing will be more interesting if they can use alternative words to express one idea, it is important for them to build up a bank of synonyms.

1 In pairs, students look up the words on the list in the dictionary and discuss possible synonyms.

Answers

1 discrepancies = *differences*
stabilize = *stop changing*
amount = *quantity*
data = *computer information*
element = *part*
converge = *come together*
figure = *number*
trends = *general patterns*
2 Suggested answers
data: *computer information*
element: a – *weather* b – *earth, water, air, fire* c – *single atom such as hydrogen*
figure: a – *important person* b – *person's shape*, c – *illustration*
trend: *a fashion*

2 Living together

Content overview

Themes

In Unit 2, students will read about and discuss topics related to the physical and mental health of teenagers across the world. Themes include self-esteem and managing personal finances, as well as social issues.

Listening
- a talk about giving up smoking
- a discussion among students about managing money

Speaking
- a sample one-minute talk from Part 2 of the IELTS Speaking module
- pronunciation practice: stress

Reading
- teenage mental and physical health

Writing
- Task 2: Argument / Opinion questions: the balanced argument approach
- paragraph planning for Writing Task 2

Exam related activities

Listening

Section 2	Note completion
	Short answers
	Matching
Section 3	Multiple choice
	Table completion

Speaking

Part 2	Describing a person
	Describing a place

Reading

Multiple choice
Summary completion from a list
True / False questions

Writing

Task 2	Balanced argument essays
	Supporting a point of view
	Paragraph planning

Language development

Language focus

Sentence subjects
Word order
Using numerical expressions
Parts of speech

Vocabulary

Collocations
Word formation: nouns and verbs
Suffixes

Skills development

Speaking

Preparing a talk by making notes

Reading

Predicting content
Skimming for genre (type of text) and purpose
Finding synonyms
Scanning for figures

Writing

Linking paragraphs
Organizing essay structures

Listening

Listening for keywords

Pronunciation

Stressed syllables

Study skills

Using a dictionary

Dictionary focus

Collocations
Suffixes

Warm up p24

Elicit vocabulary relevant to the photos at the beginning of the unit before dividing students into groups to discuss 1 and 2. Vocabulary may include: *texting, chatting, unemployed, street crime, gangs, litter.*

Listening 1 p24

Section 2

Aim
It is easier to follow a speech or conversation if we can predict the vocabulary associated with the topic. The following exercises prepare students for the IELTS Listening module by activating vocabulary in advance, encouraging students to find keywords in the questions before listening.

Ask students to brainstorm vocabulary associated with smoking. These words could be organized on the board into themes such as: *public health, personal health, ways to quit*. Ask if anyone has personal experience of giving up smoking. Discuss the advantages and disadvantages of being a non-smoker or a smoker.

Note completion

1 Ask students to look at the extract and underline the keywords (*smoker, smoking, passive, anti-social*) before completing the notes. Focus students' attention on reading the question carefully for the number of words required (see Tip on page 25).

Answers

B (C is 4 words, A is incorrect)

2 1.3 In pairs, students discuss suitable parts of speech for each space. As students may not be fully aware of word forms, explain the answers to the whole group.

Answers

1 verb – we expect *there* to be followed by *is/are/was/were* or a modal
2 verb – *to* will be followed by the basic form of the verb
3 gerund – the parallel structure leads us to expect a verb ending in *–ing*
4 and 5 plural or uncountable noun (no article suggests a plural or uncountable object noun)
6 noun – singular or plural object

Emphasize the importance of reading the questions in advance to be able to predict the main ideas before focusing on details.

Students listen to the recording once to answer questions 1–6. This will give them an idea of how well they would do in the exam. If you want to give students further listening practice, play the recording again and focus on the questions students found difficult.

Answers

1 are various methods
2 stay focused
3 phoning
4 smoking aids
5 (nicotine) withdrawal symptoms
6 your local pharmacy

1.3

Good afternoon. Welcome to *Stop Smoking Now*. You're all here today because you've decided to stop smoking. However, making the decision to stop is just the first step. Yet if you follow these guidelines, no matter how tough it may be to begin with, rest assured, you will be on your way to becoming what you want to be, an ex-smoker. The first thing to remember is that there is not only one way. What I'll give you today are various methods you can choose from. They all work and they can all help.

The first method I would recommend is based on something we all have, but in different degrees, namely willpower.

Of course just making the decision to stop is an enormous act of willpower alone, but what exactly does this mean? It means having a strong mind, waking up every morning and telling yourself that you will not have that cigarette no matter how much you may want one. To do this successfully you really have to be determined to stay focused. You need to be in the right frame of mind. But this isn't as easy as it may sound and it may mean doing other things to take your mind off having that cigarette, particularly when the urge is strong. I've found that different things can help you do this like taking up a hobby or having a smoking buddy – someone you can phone up when the going gets tough, a friend who can help you think about something else. Remember that each time you don't have a cigarette, you will feel better and stronger.

Of course, this method does not work for everyone, but there are other ways to help keep you on track.

Another way is to use smoking aids. There are many types, so find one that suits you best. Take for example nicotine patches. You put one on every day and it gives you a controlled nicotine dose. Basically, you keep reducing the amount until your body stops craving nicotine. As your body gets used to less nicotine, you may experience withdrawal symptoms. Don't worry about feeling embarrassed people will notice because many nicotine patches are see-through. So where do you get them? Well, you can buy them from your local pharmacy or supermarket. You can also ask your GP for a prescription.

Matching

2 1.4 Remind students that they must listen carefully for distracters and parallel expressions in true/false questions. In questions 7–10, students must look out for:

7 50/15, 90/19
8 *won't* put on weight
9 takes harmful toxins ... out of ...
10 from the inside

Answers

7 N
8 N
9 Y
10 Y

1.4

Another method that is becoming more popular is alternative therapies. Giving up smoking is not only difficult for your body, but also your mind as the emotional stress can be really severe. One therapy that springs to mind is acupuncture. This can help you relax, calm you down, making you are much more likely not to want to give up. Acupuncture usually lasts between 50 to 90 minutes. As your body and mind become stronger, you should need fewer sessions. The good thing about acupuncture is that it takes harmful toxins caused by smoking out of your body. And, I'm sure you'll all like this, it does not increase your appetite, so giving up smoking using this method means you won't put on weight! It can take as few as five acupuncture sessions to cure you, but of course, this depends on the type of person you are. I suppose one of the biggest advantages of using this method is that there are almost no withdrawal symptoms because it works from the inside. What I mean by this, is that acupuncture takes away your wanting to smoke and this feeling, on top of the feeling of calmness, stays with you after the treatment is over.

At the end of the day, it doesn't really matter which method you choose. What's important is that you make the decision and then stick to it no matter what. If you give up, think of the money you'll be saving! There is no better time to start than today. You can kick the habit for good!

Speaking p25

Part 2: Making notes

Aim
Active student participation in seminar discussions is an important characteristic of UK university study. Students are often required to lead seminars from papers they have prepared. Basic presentation skills are tested in Part 2 of the IELTS Speaking module.

1 Students give examples of older people who have had an influence on their lives. Brainstorm vocabulary for describing people. Focus more on personality than physical appearance. Vocabulary may include: *adventurous, brave, clever, intelligent, kind, thoughtful, generous, interesting, creative.*

Exam tip: Remind students again of the importance of making notes before giving their talk. Notes will help them cover all the points on the topic card and remember what they have planned to say, especially if they are nervous.

2 1.5 Students listen to the recording and answer 1–5 individually before discussing their answers in small groups.

Answers

1 Yes, the student attempts to do this, but not successfully.
2 No. The student starts talking about an older person and then goes off topic and begins discussing books.
3 Yes.
4 Tried to use discourse markers. Gave support for the answer (reasons).
5 Keeping to the topic. Giving more details. Varying discourse markers more. Used *actually* too often.

1.5

[E = Examiner; S = Student]

E: Now I'm going to give you a topic and I want you to speak about it for one to two minutes. First you have one minute to think about what you are going to say and you can make some notes.

Here is your topic. I want you to describe an older person who has had an influence on your life. OK?

S: Um ... well, I think a person who had most influence is probably my grandfather. He is important for me. He always help me. I did not meet him really because he is my grandfather so actually he was always in my life. Really, we did many things together. He play with me always and sometimes read me story. Actually I like reading books because it can help me to relax. Um ... I'm reading a good book now. It's about this woman and she remember her life ...er ... Actually, it's a bit of a love story, but I'm liking it very much.

3 In pairs, students discuss vocabulary for describing places. Vocabulary may include: *countryside, city, village, farm, house, flat, garden, patio, brick, wood, tiles, detached, semi-detached, terraced.* Students make notes for the talk. Students can use 1–5 in Exercise 2 as a checklist when listening to and evaluating each other's talk.

Listing 2 p27

Section 3

Elicit vocabulary to describe the spending habits of the person in the picture. Vocabulary may include: *clothes, shoes, CDs, music, drink, going out, concerts, travelling, fast food, cinema, theatre, presents, mobile phone.*

In pairs, students respond to 1 and 2. They interview each other and discuss their different priorities and preferences.

Multiple choice

1 1.6 Before listening to the recording, students highlight keywords in the stems for questions 1–4. Students predict possible answers without looking at the options (A–C). Students can then check their predictions with the options.

Answers

1 B
2 C
3 B
4 A

1.6

[S = Student]

S 1: Hi there, Sang Min. What have you been up to?

S 2: I've just been to a tutorial. Weren't you two supposed to attend?

S 3: Yes, we were, but I had an essay to finish and Juliane offered to help.

S 1: Did we miss much?

S 2: Well, I thought it was quite interesting. Er ... it was all about spending habits among undergraduates. It was based on recent research done by a PhD student studying behavioural psychology.

S 1: Oh yes, I remember being interviewed by him about what I usually spend my money on.

S 2: And what did you say?

S 1: Well, most of my money, probably around 75%, goes on <u>basic living:</u> paying rent, food costs and of course, university fees.

S 3: I'm the same, except my food bill is higher!

S 2: We are all in the same boat here. Virtually all my money goes on that too, but I also spend a lot of money on textbooks, between £100 and £120 a month, usually more. Realistically, it's closer to £150.

S 1: That explains why you get such good marks! Another aspect of the interview was students' use of credit cards, with a particular focus on how students manage these.

S 3: In my case, not very well! I always end up spending more than I planned to. It's too easy to use.

S 2: Surely that must be the point that students are given credit cards too easily before they've learnt how to use them. And the number of credit cards some students get, it's frightening. The average is about three cards.

S 1: Not only cards, students need to learn how to manage money, too. And this is what the interviews meant to find out. By comparing and contrasting all the data, the root causes of student spending could be highlighted.

S 3: And the effects this has on students, I'd imagine would be more negative than positive.

S 1: Perhaps, but this was the other part of what the student was trying to achieve. You also need to study the effects to find answers.

Table completion

2 1.7 In pairs, students discuss possible answers to questions 5–12, limiting themselves to a maximum of three words per answer.

Answers

5 resist the urge
6 practical allowance
7 Saving
8 to personal finance
9 savings account
10 participate in buying
11 their allowance/their personal allowance
12 for the rest

Suggested alternatives: 5 try not to / refuse to 6 serious discussion / spending limit 8 to financial planning / to careful spending 9 bank account 10 make financial decisions / plan their spending / decide for themselves 11 their pocket money / monthly allowance 12 for luxuries / extra expenses

1.7

[S = Student]

S 1: But I think it all goes back to how we were taught to manage money when we were children.

S 3: That's true. Our behaviour now is closely related to the childhood environment and what we learnt from that.

S 2: But how far back should we go? When do children really begin forming an understanding of what money means?

S 3: I've read that children between three and five can understand what's right and wrong. That's when they can learn concepts like sharing. At the age of six, most children can understand the value of money.

S 1: This suggests that if parents offered practical advice to their children at an early age, it could have a very positive impact on their spending habits in later life.

S 2: It basically comes down to three areas. The first one is allowance. Parents should not try to focus on how much money they give their children, but rather on what they need.

S 3: Needs are difficult to define so parents need to resist the urge to give in when their children say, *I want*.

S 1: For me, the only way to teach children the difference between needs and wants, is to give them a practical allowance. If my parents had not done that for me when I was younger, I don't think I would be able to handle the money they give me now.

S 2: Mmm ... true. The second thing I think is important is saving.

S 3: Can you explain a bit more?

S 2: Basically, parents need to introduce their children to personal finance. If we are expected to deal with money now, then we have to learn when we're younger.

S 3: I see what you mean. And it could be in quite simple ways like by helping them to open their own savings account.

S 1: There's one more area I think is vital.

S 2: What's that?

S 1: It's buying. We spend excessively on credit cards because we don't know how to control money. We almost need to learn how and what to buy, which is why parents should allow their children to participate in this. If they want something expensive like a new pair of trainers, then they could be encouraged to save a bit of their allowance.

S 3: And parents could also promise to help by saying that they will pay the rest if the child, at the end of their period of saving, still does not have enough.

Reading p28

Aim

Students at all university levels must be able to read, summarize and paraphrase academic texts in their writing. Summary completion exercises practise scanning for detail, and looking for synonyms and parallel expressions. These are both fundamental skills for paraphrasing.

1 Brainstorm teenage problems to activate related vocabulary, which may include: *drugs, loneliness, exams, sex, drinking, bullying, violence, peer pressure.*

2 After pair discussions, students answer questions 1 and 2 individually. For further practice of distinguishing text type and purpose, refer students to Photocopiable 2, Exercises 2 and 3 (TB pages 107–108).

Answers

1 C
2 D

3 After finding what the numbers in 1–5 refer to in the passage, students compare their answers with a partner.

Answers

1 ages of children studied
2 percentage of Portuguese children who start the day with a meal
3 number of countries involved in the study
4 number of children counselled by *Childline*
5 average number of children studied who saw peers as kind/helpful

Summary completion: From a list

4 Students discuss possible answers to 1 and 2.

Answers

1 better than, worse than, comparable to
2 comparable to

5 In pairs, students discuss possible word forms. Review with the whole class.

Answers

1 comparative adjective
2 number, fraction or percentage
3 size adjective
4 number or fraction
5 noun
6 noun
7 number, fraction or percentage
8 adjective
9 verb
10 verb

6 Students complete the summary.

Answers

1 comparable to
2 a fifth
3 the youngest
4 a quarter
5 peers
6 studies
7 half
8 less
9 find
10 affect

True, False, Not Given

7 Students write their answers to questions 11–15.

Answers

11 Not Given (no comparison of Scottish and English teenagers)
12 True (wide range of factors)
13 True (there is more that could be done to protect young people)
14 False (*It would also help to have a ban on …*)
15 Not Given (passage only mentions 11-year-olds)

Language focus p31

Aim
As sentences in academic texts tend to be complex and dense in content, it is essential for students to be able to recognize the subjects and verbs of all principle and subordinate clauses.

Further practice

Revise parts of speech by referring students to the exercises in Unit 2 Grammar, pages 170–171.

Sentence subjects

This section focuses on word order in English sentences. Refer students to Unit 2 Grammar, pages 170–171 for detailed revision notes.

1 and 2 Students complete the exercises individually and compare their answers with a partner.

Answers

Exercise 1
1 The survey (s), is conducted (v)
2 It (s), is (v)
3 The children (s), were asked (v)
4 Childline (s), counselled (v)
5 English youngsters (s), have (v)
6 Attitudes, behaviour and lifestyle (s), influence (v)

Exercise 2
1 The most important thing children need from their parents is love.
2 Many parenting strategies that work at one age stop working with adolescents.
3 Physical affection, love and praise from parents are important.
4 Behaviours and attitudes learned at an early age can have a lifelong effect.

Sentence subjects reporting numerical information and comparisons

Aim
An important skill in academic writing is to be able to interpret information in diagrams and graphs and to convert it into coherent text to be incorporated in essays and dissertations.

3 Students will not need to solve difficult mathematical problems for the IELTS exam but they will need some familiarity with the more basic ways of expressing and reporting information numerically. Give students time to practise saying the fractions, percentages and expressions in pairs.

Answers

1 33.3%
2 66.6%
3 50%
4 25%
5 75%
6 60%
7 70%

4 Students may benefit from doing the completion exercise (5) before attempting their own sentences in Exercise 4. Revise qualifying expressions. Refer students to Box A in Exercise 5. Explain that *less* is used with uncountable nouns and *fewer* with countable nouns. Elicit examples from the class.

5 Students complete the sentences with expressions from Box A and Box B.

Answers

1 *Half as many* Estonian girls as boys smoke.
2 There are *five times as many* girls who smoke in Greenland as (there are) in Lithuania.
3 The number of boys who smoke in Greenland is *double* that in Estonia.
4 In France, *the same* number of boys and girls smoke.
5 *Twice as many* teenagers smoke in Greenland as do in Finland.

6 Comparative structures can be difficult for students to master. This exercise gives students the opportunity to produce their own comparative sentences. Encourage students to practise a range of structures and exchange their sentences with a partner to correct and discuss differences and alternatives.

Further practice

For further practice of sentence subjects, refer students to Photocopiable 2, Exercise 1 (TB page 107).

Vocabulary 1 p33

Social issues

Aim
The use of correct collocations in academic writing improves accuracy, and allows the writer to express complex concepts more fluently and clearly. Critical thinking, the fundamental approach to learning in UK universities, is supported by the problem/solution format for discussion and writing, revisited in this section.

Further practice

Refer students to Unit 2 Vocabulary, Exercise 1, page 179.

1

Answers

1 g
2 e
3 i
4 c
5 b
6 h
7 a
8 j
9 f

2 Students discuss answers in pairs.

Suggested issues

1 Money: low income, personal debt
2 Health: cost and quality of health care
3 Family: care of the elderly, breakdown of the extended family
4 Social groups: juvenile delinquency, homophobia

3 Remind students of the problem / solution / evaluation pattern in essay questions. Point out that the solution to a problem may create a new problem which needs evaluation and a further solution.

Ask students to make brief notes about a social problem in their country before describing it to their partner.

Vocabulary 2 p33

Word formation: Nouns and verbs

Explain the addition of suffixes to change word forms. Elicit examples of nouns having the most common endings.

1 Point out that when verbs are formed from nouns, it may be necessary to make some spelling changes.

Answers

1 apply
2 associate
3 communicate
4 concentrate
5 direct
6 educate
7 examine
8 form
9 inform
10 instruct
11 operate
12 organize
13 populate
14 produce
15 react
16 relate
17 situate
18 vary

2 Students underline the stressed syllables. Observe that for words ending in *-tion* the stress falls on the second syllable from the end.

Answers

1 appli'cation /ap'ply
2 associ'ation / as'sociate
3 communi'cation / com'municate
4 concen'tration / 'concentrate
5 di'rection / di'rect
6 edu'cation / 'educate
7 examin'ation / e'xamine
8 for'mation / form
9 infor'mation / in'form
10 in'struction / in'struct
11 oper'ation / 'operate
12 organi'zation / 'organize
13 popu'lation / 'populate
14 pro'duction / pro'duce
15 re'action / re'act
16 re'lation / re'late
17 situ'ation / 'situate
18 vari'ation / 'vary

3 1.8 Play the recording for students to check their answers. In pairs, students practise saying the nouns and verbs in Exercise 1.

1.8

1 appli'cation /ap'ply 2 associ'ation / as'sociate 3 communi'cation / com'municate 4 concen'tration / 'concentrate 5 di'rection / di'rect 6 edu'cation / 'educate 7 examin'ation / e'xamine 8 for'mation / form 9 infor'mation / in'form 10 in'struction / in'struct 11 oper'ation / 'operate 12 organi'sation / 'organize 13 popu'lation / 'populate 14 pro'duction / pro'duce 15 re'action / re'act 16 re'lation / re'late 17 situ'ation / 'situate 18 vari'ation / 'vary

4

Answers

1 reaction
2 formation
3 production
4 relations
5 education
6 operated
7 situated
8 examination
9 applications

Writing p34

Task 2

Aim
One of the most important skills in academic study is the ability to analyse an essay title and to respond appropriately to it. Students often have difficulty distinguishing between the main topic and the specific aspect of the topic to be discussed. They must also be able to express their viewpoint clearly in discursive writing.

1 Ask students to find the answers to 1–5 in the Introduction on pages 4–7 and discuss any doubts in their group. Any unresolved questions can be clarified in a whole group session.

Answers

1 250 words
2 40 minutes, it is worth two thirds of the marks
3 Task Response, Coherence and Cohesion, Lexical Resource, Grammatical Range and Accuracy
4 A response to a given opinion or problem
5 Suggested structure: Introduction, Development, Conclusion
Steps involved in writing an essay: Thinking and Planning, Writing and Checking

Understanding the question

2 Explain that each essay title has four parts: *the topic, the focus, the viewpoint* and *the task*. The topic is the most general theme, the focus is a specific aspect/part or influence on that theme, the viewpoint may be established in the title or may be required of the writer and the task tells the writer what type of essay he/she is expected to write (for example problem/solution, discussion/opinion, criticism, description).

Answers

1 and 4 are instructions

2 is the statement

3 is the task

3

Answers

1 no
2 only if the habits are a cause of stress
3 not in detail but your experience can be part of your evidence
4 no
5 yes
6 yes (opinion + arguments)

4

Answers

Topics are underlined, tasks are in bold italics.

1 *The age at which children are allowed to work for money (topic) varies from country to country. While some people believe it is wrong, others regard it as a valuable opportunity to gain experience of the work environment.*

Discuss the arguments for and against (task) *children participating in paid work.*

Briefly state that the attitude to children's work varies according to culture and law. Describe the arguments for and against. Conclude with a summary and your own opinion.

2 *These days, the wealthy in society often throw away perfectly good products in order to replace them with more up-to-date models.*

Do the ***environmental disadvantages*** *of this development outweigh the* ***economic advantages****?*

Briefly describe the 'throw-away culture' of today's consumer society. Describe the environmental costs of this, then contrast with the economic benefits. Conclude with a summary and your own opinion.

3 *Many governments state that they value equal opportunities for all but do not provide adequate support for the disabled.*

Discuss *this view and* ***give your own opinion.***

Briefly describe the idea of equal opportunity and its relevance to the disabled. Then outline the arguments for the statement (why governments are failing to provide enough support) and then outline the arguments showing how governments are succeeding. Conclude with a summary and your own opinion.

Argument/Opinion Questions 1: The Balanced Argument Approach

5 Students underline the topic (*teenagers*), focus (*stressful*), viewpoint (*more ... than previous generations*) and task (*discuss ... and give your opinion*) in the essay question in Exercise 2 and compare their answers with a partner.

Students then make a note of their arguments supporting and contradicting the statement, and discuss them with their partner.

6 Students complete 1–5.

Using the arguments they discussed in Exercise 5, students write a paragraph each for statements i–v.

Answers

3 the body of the essay
4 No, not necessarily. Select those that are strongest and that you have sufficient vocabulary to describe.
5 one main idea which may be supported by other ideas

7

Answers

Three main ideas:
1 exposed to more products than earlier generations (films/media, youth-oriented advertizing)
2 pressure to succeed at school (achieve lifestyle in media, compete for best jobs, parental pressure)
3 stresses in earlier times (hunger, physical hardship)

8 Linking expressions are reviewed in detail in Unit 8 Language focus, page 124; Unit 8 Grammar, page 176 and Unit 9 Dictionary focus, page 151.

Revise the functions of the linking words in the box. Students could complete the box with the words from Exercise 9 before adding the words from the box to the correct place in the essay.

Answers

1 as a result of
2 In addition
3 Consequently
4 In order to
5 so
6 On the other hand
7 for example
8 Nevertheless

9

Answers

1 contrast/concession = *although, while, in spite (of)*
2 reasons = *because, due to*
3 further support = *furthermore, moreover*
4 examples = *such as, for instance*
5 result/consequence = *therefore, thus*
6 purpose = *such as to* + infinitive

10

Answers

1 Firstly, On the other hand, To sum up,
2 In addition, Consequently, Nevertheless
3 Despite, as a result of, In order to, so, although

11

Answers

1 Longest = *peer pressure to conform by owning the latest designer-label clothing + produces.* Other long sentence subjects = *life for modern teenagers + is, youth-oriented advertising + makes, Parental pressure, exams and homework + are (all) reported, hunger and physical discomfort + would (undoubtedly) have caused, consumerism and academic pressure + are*
2 -tion = *generations, examinations*
-ity = *celebrities, anxiety, society*
-er = *teenagers, designer*
-ness = *awareness*
-ism = *consumerism*
-ment = *improvement, arguments*

12 Refer students to the model answer Unit 2 Writing, page 189 to discuss use of linking words and structure.

Study skills p39

Using a dictionary

1 Students discuss the advantages and disadvantages of using a monolingual dictionary.

Advantages: develop language by reading definitions in English, meanings shown in context, wider range of meanings shown

Disadvantages: definitions may use unknown vocabulary, slower

2

Answers

1 adverb
2 conjunction
3 preposition
4 infinitive
5 uncountable noun
6 transitive verb
7 somebody
8 followed by a clause beginning with *that*
9 followed by an infinitive
10 followed by verb + *-ing*

3

Answers

1 /ˈdʒʌstɪs/
2 INJUSTICE
3 social justice
4 anything in italics
5 **1a.** the fact that something is reasonable and fair

Dictionary focus p39

1

Answers

1 in sth
2 of sth
3 advice/solution/use
4 on sth/sb
5 uncontrolled
6 annoying/bad
7 express/give/offer

2 Students record word families in a table. Point out that not all words take all forms and discuss the alternatives for: *addict/become addicted to, opinion/to have an opinion.*

Students can write sentences incorporating at least two forms of each word and discuss them in small groups.

Answers

noun – object	noun – person	noun – process	verb	adjective	adverb
product	producer	production	produce	productive	productively
–	addict	addiction	–	addictive	–
–	participant	participation	participate	participative	–
–	practitioner	practise	practice	practical	practically
–	–	influence	influence	influential	influentially
–	consumer	consumerism	consume	consuming	–
habit	–	–	habituate	–	habitually
opinion	–	–	–	opinionated	–

3 Costing the earth

Content overview

Themes

Environmental issues are the main theme of Unit 3. Students will be able to bring an international perspective to texts and discussions which centre on recycling, renewable resources and the availability and use of oil and alternative fuels.

Listening

- two dialogues between a lecturer and a student about recycling and the consumer society
- a radio report on government energy policy

Reading

- oil and alternative fuels

Writing

- interpreting diagrams and graphs for Writing Task 1

Exam related activities

Listening

Section 3 Multiple choice
Summary completion

Reading

Multiple-choice questions
Matching

Writing

Task 1 Selecting significant information
Describing and comparing information in fixed time diagrams

Speaking

Part 3 Introducing an opinion and supporting it with examples

Language development

Language focus

Compound adjectives
Comparatives and superlatives

Vocabulary

Collocations
Dependent prepositions

Skills development

Reading

Guessing unknown vocabulary from context
Scanning for detailed information

Writing

Summarizing information in diagrams
Making comparisons

Listening

Listening for detail

Pronunciation

Final consonants:

/s/ /z/ /d/ /k/ /n/ /l/

Speaking

Introducing and organizing opinions

Study skills

Vocabulary for describing and comparing

Dictionary focus

Word forms

Warm up p40

Elicit the vocabulary of transport and the environment by referring students to the pictures and asking them to compare the sizes and functions of the vehicles. Vocabulary may include: *off road, high performance, fuel consumption, fast, family car, racing, formula one, sporty, 00 miles per litre/gallon*.

In small groups, students discuss the relative popularity of different vehicles in their country and compare them with others. Encourage students to give reasons and explanations for their opinions.

Reading p40

Aim
Scanning titles and subtitles for relevance to an essay title or research question can be a valuable time-saving study technique. Students can also learn to read the first sentence of each paragraph for the gist of the content.

Elicit predictions from the title and subtitle of the article about the content. Make sure students read all the words in the subtitle (*wells, high oil prices, alternative fuels*).

1, 2 and 3 Ask students to read the title of the article and answer the questions in pairs.

Answers

1 and 2 D
3 British (para. 5: *we*)

Multiple-choice questions

4 Students complete this exercise individually. Review the answers with the whole class.

Answers

1 petrol shortage/near future
2 changes/North Sea oil supplies
3 not affect/price oil
4 higher fuel prices/bring about

5 Working in pairs, students have the opportunity to discuss the details of the article before choosing responses. They will benefit from their own and their partner's errors which should make them more aware of the dangers of distracters.

Answers

1 D
2 B
3 A
4 A

Matching

6 Students complete the matching exercise and confirm their responses with their neighbour.

Answers

5 D
6 D
7 H
8 O
9 P or D
10 P or D
11 H
12 O

Dealing with unknown vocabulary in a reading passage

Aim
When students come across unknown vocabulary in academic texts, they often feel the need to understand every word and refer to the dictionary frequently. This slows down their reading significantly and limits the range of sources they can consult. Guessing meaning from context and contingent words is a very useful way to speed up reading.

7 Remind students that they cannot only guess from context but, if they speak an Indo-European language, they can look for similarities between words in their own language and English (*cognates*). For example *nascent* means *being born*. Students must also be aware that not all cognates have similar meanings. However, this shouldn't prevent them from using the technique to guess possible meanings in context.

8 In pairs, students discuss possible meanings of the expressions before looking them up in a dictionary and checking the meaning.

Suggested answers

1 finite = *limited*
2 derived from = *coming from*
3 shortage = *not enough*
4 dwindling = *getting smaller*
5 massive = *very big*
6 burgeoning = *growing*
7 initial = *at the beginning*
8 sustained = *supported, continued*

9 Explain that we do not necessarily need to know the meaning of words that are:

- examples in a list (*ore emulsion, shales, geopolitics, petrol/electric, hybrid/bio fuels*)
- between commas in non-defining relative clauses (*balance of payments*).

Language focus p44

Compound adjectives used in place of relative clauses

Aim
The use of compound adjectives and correct collocations makes academic writing more concise and accurate. This section develops students' ability to combine concepts in compound adjectives and students' awareness of collocations.

Introduce compound adjectives by asking students to find the following examples in the article on page 41: *short-sighted* (para. 5), *tax-friendly* (para. 8), *off-road* (para. 12). Students should explain the examples in their own words. This exercise should demonstrate that compound adjectives are a concise way of describing two attributes of a concept without using a lengthy relative clause.

Students can practise forming compound adjectives by completing the exercise in the Grammar section on page 172.

1 and 2 Students combine compound adjectives and nouns to replace the relative clauses and check with the text.

Answers

1 long-awaited adoption
2 wallet-friendly alternatives
3 fuel-efficient cars
4 cleaner-burning petrol and diesel engines
5 high fuel-consumption vehicles
6 new-generation vehicles

3 Students work in pairs to create compound adjectives.

Suggested answers

1 Low-lying areas are more likely to flood.
2 It is recommended to eat a well-balanced diet.
3 Ford have produced a high-performance estate car.
4 People entering and leaving the building are monitored on closed-circuit television.
5 In spite of his qualifications and experience, he was offered only short-term employment and not a permanent post.
6 Teaching and nursing have traditionally been low-paid jobs.
7 Fox hunting is a long-standing British tradition.
8 We prefer to do business with well-established companies.

For a more detailed grammatical explanation refer students to Unit 3 Grammar, pages 171–172.

Vocabulary p45

Collocations

Explain that certain words are often found together. For example ***against a background***, ***to make a sacrifice***. The correct use of collocations makes writing and speaking more fluent and accurate.

1 Explain that *energy* can be a noun or an adjective. When it is a noun, it goes after the adjective or the verb (as an object); when it is an adjective it goes in front of the noun.

Answers

1 Words typically coming before: *alternative, atomic, conserve, conventional, generate, harness, nuclear, provide, renewable, solar, sustainable, wave, wind*
2 Words typically coming after: *consumption, costs, efficiency, policy, production, requirement, shortage*

2

Answers

1 policy
2 harness
3 sustainable
4 consumption
5 requirement
6 generate
7 renewable
8 conventional

3 and 4 1.9 Explain that the text for completion is the transcript of a brief radio report on government energy policy. Students will listen to it to check their answers.

Students complete the text.

Play the recording for correction. Words used for completion are underlined in the recording script below.

Answers

1 harnessing (gerund because it follows *for*)
2 renewable/sustainable (*renewable* is normally an adjective, but has recently become a plural noun, *renewables,* meaning *renewable sources of energy)*
3 renewable/sustainable
4 generate
5 requirements
6 consumption
7 conventional

1.9

The Department of Energy denied claims that a change in its energy policy is being debated in light of fresh evidence of global warming. A government minister denied that a decision has been taken to back technologies for harnessing the power of renewable and sustainable sources of energy such as wind and solar power. The Department claims that renewables are unable to generate enough power to meet growing energy requirements economically. Campaigners for the environment point out that given the predicted steep rise in energy consumption it is more important than ever that the government takes steps to reduce demands for conventional sources of energy, like fossil fuels, which are damaging to the environment.

Further practice

For extended revision of word forms, ask students to complete Unit 3 Vocabulary, Exercise 2, page 180.

Listening p46

Section 3: Multiple choice

Aim
At a UK university a considerable amount of time is spent listening to academic discourse in the form of lectures, seminars and discussions. As it is usual for ideas to be rephrased and reformulated during a discussion, it is important for students to listen for synonyms and parallel expressions.

Brainstorm key vocabulary related to waste and recycling. Ask students to classify vocabulary into categories related to: household, commercial and industrial waste, recycling and renewable. Elicit students' experiences of recycling, encouraging them to describe and compare local and national policies.

1

Answers

1 b
2 d
3 c
4 a

2 Students discuss and answer 1–6.

Answers

1 yes
2 no
3 because she isn't worried about missing the lecture
4 she knows it fairly well
5 because she knows her subject well
6 worried

3 1.10 Play the recording and ask students to answer questions 1–4.

Students compare their answers in pairs and discuss any differences. The correct answers are underlined in the recording script below.

Answers

1 B
2 B
3 C
4 A

1.10

[Dr D = Dr Dartford; M = Miranda]

Dr D: Good afternoon, Dr Dartford speaking.

M: Good afternoon, Doctor. It's Miranda Smith here.

Dr D: Oh, hello Miranda. How can I help you?

M: I'm really sorry, but I couldn't come to your lecture on the government's waste strategy yesterday because I was feeling ill. My essay has to be handed in in two weeks' time and I'm worried I might have missed something important. I really don't like it when I miss lectures, especially when I need the information for an essay.

Dr D: Well, try not to worry. You can't help being sick. How about if I give you a quick summary of the main points?

M: That'd be great, thanks. Just let me get a pen. Right, I'm ready.

Dr D: To begin with, I stressed the importance of us re-using and recycling waste in the future. I made particular reference to the UK which at the moment only recycles about eight per cent of household waste. The levels of industrial and commercial waste are much higher. It's frightening how much waste factories produce on a daily basis, but that's not all. The fact is that not only is this rate of recycling well below government targets, but it's at a much lower rate than many other European countries which means Britain is just not keeping pace with the rate of growth in household waste.

M: That's pretty worrying, isn't it?

Dr D: It certainly is. What is more, we need to understand that if we are to achieve a more rational and sustainable use of our resources in this country, then we have to develop a fundamental change in the way we think about waste.

M: That won't be easy. What suggestions did you propose?

Dr D: Just give me a second, let me check my notes. OK, got it. Basically, there are a couple of ways this could be achieved. One of these is for more household waste to be separated.

M: You mean separated into things like newspapers, tins and stuff like that?

Dr D: Yes, that's the idea. Then this separated waste would obviously need different forms of collection by local councils, but most importantly, it will require an expansion in the market for collected materials, which is one of the major barriers to increased recycling. New government targets have also been set for recycling or composting 30 per cent of household waste by 2010.

M: But that's almost a fourfold increase, isn't it?

Dr D: It is indeed. Rather a frightening figure, whichever way you look at it.

Summary completion

4 1.11 Ask students to read the passage in pairs and guess possible answers. Remind them that they must not use more than three words in their answer.

After listening to the recording, students compare their predictions with the correct answers.

Answers

5 general public
6 lifestyle
7 ready-made meals
8 be more convenient
9 throw-away culture
10 consumers

1.11

[Dr D = Dr Dartford; M = Miranda]

Dr D: As you say, it's a fourfold increase, but my guess is it won't stop there. You must remember the previous government found that setting targets is one thing, but if the practical policies are not in place, nothing will happen.

M: So what is the government planning to do about all this waste?

Dr D: Well, apparently they're going to publish a final strategy setting out a range of policies to start and sustain the necessary changes. But the interesting part for me was that it's not only up to the government. To say we need more recycling is a simple message, but, and here is the crux of the matter, there's another one that isn't getting enough attention.

M: Really? What's that?

Dr D: It's quite obvious really, it's us, the general public. We have to reduce the amount of waste we make. It's our responsibility. Did you know that every hour, enough waste is produced to fill the Sydney Opera House? And the rate is increasing.

M: Actually, now you mention it, I remember reading somewhere that the reason for all this waste is our increasing wealth and the changes to our lifestyles. I guess it's quite obvious when you really think about it, I mean it's things like shops and supermarkets selling more pre-packaged foods and ready-made meals.

Dr D: Convenience is the key. People simply want their lives to be more convenient and there's also technological change that brings pressure to make people change their domestic appliances for newer models.

M: I never thought about that, but you're right. And I'm just as guilty. I threw out my old stereo so I could have a better model even though there wasn't really anything wrong with the old one.

Dr D: You see, you're a classic example that changing our present 'throw-away' culture is going to be an enormous challenge. At the end of the day, consumers will have an important role to play. It could all boil down to their choices and their willingness to support recycling by sorting their waste and accepting more recycled products.

5 Students write a sentence for each of the expressions in 1–4. When they have found synonyms in the dictionary, they can rephrase their original sentences and compare and discuss them with a partner.

Suggested answers

(accept any reasonable suggestions)
1 an increasing tendency
2 refuse from industries and businesses
3 products already wrapped or in a box at the time of sale
4 temporary depression in economic prosperity on a global scale

Pronunciation p48

Final consonants

Point out that elision is a feature of pronunciation in which sounds at the end of one word merge with the beginning of another, for example *law (a)n(d) order, nex(t) please*. If students do not know how to join their speech in this way, they will still be understood. However if final consonants are not pronounced at all, communication may be affected. For example *We must hand in our essay(s) by 3.30 on Friday*. (If the final s is not pronounced, it isn't clear that there is more than one essay to hand in.)

1 1.12 Students work with a partner to practise the pronunciation of the final consonant sounds and place them in the correct category. Play the recording for students to check their answers.

Answers

/s/ importance, targets, convenience, appliance, recycles
/z/ policies, propose
/d/ household
/k/ public, domestic
/n/ solution, sustain
/l/ futile, conventional, fundamental, sustainable

2 1.13 Students work with a partner to practise the pronunciation of the sentences, correcting each other where necessary. Students check their answers with the recording.

1.13

1 The UK has less recycled household waste and rather more industrial and commercial waste.
2 The government needs to start and sustain changes in refuse collection.
3 The general public needs to think more about recycling and develop a fundamental change in the way they get rid of their domestic waste.
4 He made the suggestion that a sustainable solution required an expansion in the market.

Speaking p49

Aim
The discussion of controversial issues is an important part of academic life. Through contact with other students and staff, students will be exposed to a wide range of cultural and intellectual experiences. The ability to define terms, compare and contrast ideas and defend opinions is central to this environment of discussion.

1

Answers

Possible answers for 1 are that in an exam situation:
- the conversation is unnatural
- the examiner does not ask authentic questions (he/she does not need the information)
- the examiner does not ask questions to clarify misunderstandings
- the candidate is expected to continue speaking uninterrupted for up to two minutes and to give full answers to all questions
- the candidate does not ask questions

The answer to 2 is that the language used in the IELTS Speaking module should be formal without being technical.

Speaking practice: Part 3 Introducing and organizing your opinions

Aim
In Part 3 of the IELTS Speaking module, candidates are expected to give an opinion about a topic of general interest and discuss it with the examiner. Candidates may be asked to trace the history of a situation (past), describe the current situation (present) and/or predict future developments. Candidates need to support their opinions with examples and explanations.

2 Write the following statements on the board:

The government needs to start and sustain changes in refuse collection.

The general public needs to think more about recycling and develop a fundamental change in the way they get rid of their domestic waste.

Elicit opinions from students on each of these statements and illustrate the three stepping stones: sentence starters, main ideas and supporting ideas (explanations, examples).

3 Ask students to give opinions in a variety of ways by completing the sentence starters (Introducing your opinions) from the Useful language box. Students can give an opinion on the following, or any other, controversial statement about energy:

The world would be better off if all cars were banned.

Students support their opinions with examples by completing the remaining sentence starters (Extra information ...).

4 In pairs, students match phrases from the Useful language box to the main ideas. Encourage students to develop a discussion.

Suggested answers

1 For example in the UK, North Sea oil and gas are running out.
2 One example that springs to mind is giving council tax reductions to people who recycle their rubbish.
3 For instance, nuclear waste is impossible to dispose of.
4 Probably the best example I can think of is the way we buy new electronic equipment instead of repairing it.

5 Before speaking, students make brief notes of their main ideas and supporting examples for 1–3. They should then form small groups to discuss the issues.

Writing p50

Task 1

Aim
It is important for students to be able to transfer information from diagrams to written text. This section gives students practice in selecting, describing, analysing and comparing relevant data.

1 Students prepare for a small group discussion by making brief notes to answer 1–3. One member of each group should keep a record of the main points of the discussion and report back to the whole class.

2 Students should underline the keywords in the question (*car drivers, two types of fuel, different age groups, 2005*). Remind students that this graph shows a comparison at a fixed point in time so they will not use the language of trends.

Task 1: Selecting significant information

3

Answers

3, 2, 4, 1

4

Answers

1 The highest consumption is for the middle age groups with less for the younger and older age ranges. Also, overall consumption of unleaded is higher than diesel.
2 Unleaded petrol.
3 the 20–25 year age group
4 the 51–55 and 56–60 age groups (where more diesel is consumed)
5
- looking at the highest and lowest uses, and biggest differences
- looking at the pattern for Unleaded first, then the pattern for Diesel
- looking at each age group in turn

5 Remind students that an introduction should include:
- a paraphrase of the title or a general comment describing the main elements of the graph
- a comment on the most significant patterns, with numerical support

Answers

B (Diagram is introduced with a paraphrase of the question. Main feature described and supported with figures.)

Suggested reasons why A is weaker:
- There is no introductory sentence.
- It lacks numerical precision.
- It uses inappropriate register.
- It misinterprets the diagram. The writer says that *consumption increased from ... to*. This is incorrect as the diagram shows differences in one fixed time, not changes across different times.
- The answer gives a suggestion for the pattern, which is inappropriate for Task 1. In Task 1 only a factual description is required.

Suggested reasons why C is weaker:
The first sentence is a copy not a paraphrase.

Further practice

For further writing practice comparing data in charts, refer students to Photocopiable 3 (TB page 109).

Task 1: Fixed time diagrams

6 Explain that students are required to summarize the main points of the model answer in note form, and use their own words. This is easier if they work in pairs and then review the answers as a whole class.

Suggested answers

Point 1: main patterns/contrasts
Point 2: the greatest difference is for the 20–25 age group
Point 3: 51–60 age groups show a different pattern
Point 4: diesel use the same for the older age groups
Point 5: (single sentence summarizing the overall trend) differences between age groups
Point 6: middle age groups highest consumers

Point out the use of the present and the past tense in this type of question. When the writer is describing the graph itself he/she will use the present tense, for example *The 20–25 year range **shows** the largest variation in fuel use ...* (para. 2). But as the data is taken from the past, the writer has the option of using the past tense when describing the data, for example ... *unleaded petrol **was consumed** at a higher rate...* (para. 1).

7 Revise comparative and superlative structures, referring to the table on pages 52–53 before asking students to complete the exercise.

Answers

comparatives = 1, 2, 3, 5, 7, 8
superlatives = 0, 4, 6

1 D, C
2 C, B
3 B, A
4 A
5 C, D
6 E
7 C, D
8 E

8 Point out that the first sentence is a general comment about road and rail travel and that the second sentence gives more specific detail.

Refer students to the table on pages 52–53 and ask them to write one general and one specific sentence about each of the diagrams before discussing their sentences in pairs.

Suggested answers

1 Germany and Russia consume similar amounts of oil. Russia uses 949 m barrels, slightly less than Germany's 985 m barrels.
2 There is a marked contrast between CO_2 emissions in the North and the South. The South produces over twice as much CO_2 as the North.
3 Nearly half the electricity produced in Europe is generated by Britain, Sweden and Belgium. The largest producer of the three is Britain, which supplies 26% of all electricity.
4 Both China and the USA consume significantly more steel than they produce. China consumes approximately three times as much steel as it produces, while the USA consumes roughly four times its production.

9 Students use the table on pages 52–53 to replace the comparative expressions in the model answer on page 52.

Answers

0 greater
1 in contrast to
2 the widest/the most significant
3 as great as
4 In comparison
5 a wide disparity
6 the largest amount/quantity of

For further practice, ask students to look at the fuel use table in Exercise 10 on page 54 and write their own gapped sentences comparing the data. They should use language from the table on pages 52–53. In pairs, students can swap sentences and complete each other's gaps.

Task 1: further practice

10 Students work in pairs to answer 1–3. Check answers with the whole class.

Answers

1 percentage of fuel used to produce electricity
2 Belgium and Sweden highest for nuclear use with Italy having none. Germany and Britain similar use of coal and lignite, and much higher than other countries. Italy had by far the greatest proportion of petroleum products. Sweden produces almost half of its electricity from hydro and wind – over twice that of Italy. The remaining countries using it only very little. Significant use of other fuels.
3 Two possibilities: by fuel type or by country. Students should use the way they find easiest.

Study skills p55

Recording vocabulary for Writing Task 1

1 Refer students to Unit 1 Writing, Exercise 4, page 19 to revise language for describing changes over time, and to Unit 3, Writing, Exercise 6, page 53 to revise language of comparison at a fixed time.

Students then complete the table by matching the expressions with their functions in Task 1 answers.

Answers

Introductory phrases to Writing Task 1	Describing overall trends or features	Describing changes over time	Making comparisons
The given data illustrates ... *This table/graph/chart clearly shows ...*	*The USA consumes the greatest proportion of energy.* *In general, the most significant change occurred in ...*	*A fluctuated considerably from ... to ...* *The exception to this trend is/was ...*	*A and B experienced an identical increase.* *A was over twice as large as B.*

Dictionary focus p55

1 and 2 Students discuss the word forms and possible meanings of the words in the context of the reading text, before checking in the dictionary and adding the words to their vocabulary bank.

4 Healthy body, healthy mind

Content overview

Themes

In Unit 4, students will discuss personal and social perspectives on health issues. Topics include diet, nutrition, illness, medical treatment, health care and food production.

Listening
- a lecture on tiredness

Reading
- the benefits of eating chocolate
- self-help and health care

Writing
- argument / opinion essays for Writing Task 2

Exam related activities

Listening

Section 4	Note completion
	Multiple choice
	Summary completion

Reading

Matching headings
Table completion
Short answer questions
Multiple choice
True / False

Writing

Task 2	Planning paragraph structures for argument / opinion essays

Speaking

Part 2	Describing and discussing food
Part 3	Giving opinions about food

Language development

Language focus

Defining and non-defining relative clauses
Past and present participle clauses (*-ed* / *-ing*)

Vocabulary

Medical terms
Suffixes

Skills development

Reading

Skimming for purpose and organization
Scanning for detail
Scanning for argument

Writing

Generating ideas through perspective
Expressing opinions

Listening

Listening for detail
Prediction

Speaking

Introducing and organizing opinions

Study skills

Brainstorming, mind maps

Dictionary focus

Word forms

Warm up p56

In the UK the National Health Service (NHS) is the state-financed health provider, offering free treatment to all members of the EU. To elicit vocabulary related to health and medicine, ask students about the health services in their country. Vocabulary may include: *hospital, clinic, emergency, maternity, private, public/state, intensive care, surgery, operating theatre.*

Speaking p56

1 and 2 Brainstorm vocabulary for food groups and healthy / unhealthy habits. Vocabulary may include: *saturated/unsaturated fat, fibre, smoking, drinking, junk food, working out, cycling, walking, jogging.*

Students make notes individually before discussing the questions in small groups.

Reading 1 p57

Aim
Students will often need to skim academic texts to establish the purpose and the outline of the argument. Remind students that reading the abstract at the beginning of the text will give a broad outline of the contents and the viewpoint. The first sentence of each paragraph is also a helpful guideline to the argument.

1

Answers

B

2

Answers

1 C
2 B
3 D
4 A
5 I
6 G
7 F
8 H

Completing tables, diagrams, notes

3 Students complete this exercise individually. Review in pairs. Remind students that in the IELTS exam they will lose points if they use more than two words in their response.

Answers

1 cholesterol
2 stress
3 sugar
4 blood sugar
5 lactase
6 caffeine

Short answer questions

4

Aim
When students are using academic texts, they need to distinguish between facts and opinions in source material in order to support their arguments in essays.

Before looking for the relevant words in the reading text, students underline the keywords in the questions.

Answers

7 polyphenols
8 70
9 bloating, cramping, diarrhoea
10 hypothalamus
11 (any three of) chromium, iron, magnesium, calcium

Language focus p59

Defining and non-defining relative clauses

Explain that relative clauses are used to describe and define people and ideas. They are one of the most effective ways of extending ideas and expressing complex concepts. They may contain essential (defining) information or additional (non-defining) information. They are most frequently introduced by *which, that, who.*

1 Students work individually and compare their answers with a partner.

Answers

1 Chocolate is good for people <u>who are lactose-intolerant</u>. (*who* = relative pronoun)
2 Teenagers <u>whose skin is affected by acne can safely eat chocolate</u>. (*whose* = relative pronoun)
3 Chocolate contains valeric acid, <u>which is a relaxant and tranquillizer</u>. (*which* = relative pronoun)
4 Chocolate has a reasonably low GI, <u>which means it gives a long-lasting energy</u>. (*which* = relative pronoun)

2 Students answer 1–3. They should refer to Unit 4 Grammar, pages 172–173 for a detailed explanation of defining and non-defining relative clauses.

Answers

1a who
b which
c whose
Note: It is less common to replace *who* with *that* than to replace *which* with *that*.
2a Sentences 0, 1, because the relative clauses in these sentences are defining.
b The relative pronoun could be omitted in 0, because it is the object of the relative clause.
3 Because they are non-defining clauses. They give extra, non-essential information.

3 In pairs, students answer a–c. Refer them to Unit 4 Grammar, pages 172–173 if necessary.

Answers

a defining
b defining
c non-defining

4 Students complete the gaps with the information from the box and check with a partner.

Answers

1 ,which is 75 years,
2 ,causes coughing, sneezing and a runny nose to wash out the virus.
3 which infects them
4 ,where the body temperature is lower.
5 which is more dominant
6 ,which promotes sweating and hastens healing,
7 in which/that people respond to illness
8 who panic or get distressed
9 which/that (zero) the immune system is the only cure for.

Further practice

Refer students to the exercise for Unit 4 Grammar, page 173, for additional practice. Students underline the relative pronouns before deciding if the sentences are correct or not.

Participle clauses: *-ing* and *-ed*

Refer students to Unit 4 Grammar, Participle clauses, page 173. Explain that relative clauses can be introduced by present or past participles. To decide which to use, look first at the main verb in the relative clause. If it is active, the participle will end in *-ing*. If it is passive, the past participle will be used.

Answers

1a active
1b passive

2

Answers

1 present
2 past

3 Students work individually to rewrite the sentences. They compare their answers with a partner.

Answers

1 The hypothalamus is the part of the brain *controlling hunger.*
2 Chocolate contains substances *thought to make us more alert.*
3 We need lactose to digest the sugar *found in milk.*
4 We may have more colds in the winter because we huddle together more for warmth, *making cross-infection more likely.*
5 Coughing is a reaction to the irritation in the throat *caused by colds.*
6 A cough is a rush of air through the voice box *producing a sound unique to each individual.*
7 Chocolate slows downs brain waves, *making us feel calm.*

Speaking p61

Aim
This section gives students practice in making brief notes before speaking, which is useful preparation for taking part in seminars and discussions in lectures.

1 Students make brief notes to answer 1–4 before discussing the answers as a class.

2 Students make a note of three questions about food and health. Encourage students to include a question about the past, the present and the future.

3 After talking about a popular dish from their country, students create two new task cards with questions about food and health services in their partner's country. Both students make notes and talk for one minute about the topics on the task cards.

4 Write each of the questions on separate slips of paper. Students select a slip at random and, after making notes for three minutes, lead the discussion on the chosen topic. Remind students to use the language of opinion, Unit 3, page 49.

Reading 2 p61

Following an argument in a passage

1

Answers

1 b
2 c
3 a

Multiple-choice questions: multiple answers

2 Explain that this type of question requires students to choose three correct answers from a list.

Answers

1 A B D
2 A B F

3 Ask students to decide whether sentences 3–5 give factual information or opinions.

Answers

3 fact
4 opinion
5 fact

4 Individually, students underline the keywords in each question. Working in pairs, they scan the text to find the keywords, synonyms and / or parallel expressions that express the writer's opinion.

Answers

6 Yes (para. 9)
7 No (para. 4)
8 Not Given
9 Yes (para. 5)
10 Yes (para. 8)
11 Not Given
12 A

Vocabulary p64

Medical terms

1, 2 and 3 Students discuss their experiences of illness and related symptoms, and complete the table. Go through the answers with the whole class.

Answers

1 f: 1, 2, 4
2 d: 1, 2, 3, 6
3 e: 1, 2, 5, 6
4 b: 1, 2
5 a: 2

Further practice

Refer students to Unit 4 Vocabulary, Exercises 1 and 2, page 181.

Writing 1 p64

Task 2: Essay sections

Aim
An awareness of discourse markers is an invaluable aid to determining the logical structure of a text and allows students to identify the main thesis, focus, supporting points, examples and writer's point of view.

1 Explain that certain phrases or discourse markers in a text act as signposts to guide the reader through the writer's argument.

Individually, students underline the organizing, or signpost, words in the extracts (1 A further point 2 To conclude 3 For instance 4 The focus of this essay) before deciding to which part of the essay each extract relates.

Answers

Sentence 1: Body
Sentence 2: Conclusion
Sentence 3: Body
Sentence 4: Introduction

Paragraph structure: The body of the essay

Aim
A clearly structured paragraph is more accessible to the reader and communicates ideas effectively. At advanced academic levels, writers will structure complex paragraphs to reflect complex lines of argument. However, under the time and word limits of IELTS Writing Task 2, it is more practical to follow a relatively simple paragraph format, which allows the reader to identify the main idea, the development of this idea in the form of explanation or examples, and a concluding or transition sentence which leads into the following paragraph.

2 Students match the explanations to the appropriate sections of the plan.

Answers

1 B
2 D
3 C
4 A

3 Ask students to underline the discourse markers and to use them to identify the function of each sentence in the paragraph.

Answers

sentence 1 = development
sentence 2 = opposing idea
sentence 3 = development
sentence 4 = main idea
sentence 5 = paragraph conclusion

Explain the following and ask students to rewrite the paragraph.

These foods (sentence 1): refers back to *processed food*
However (sentence 2): opposing idea
Furthermore (sentence 3): further information
The first point (sentence 4): introducing main idea
Nevertheless (sentence 5): contrasting idea after a concession

Model paragraph

The first point to consider is the link between the consumption of processed food and obesity. These foods are often high in sugar and fat, both of which can lead to weight gain. Furthermore, many nutrients are lost from processed food during preparation making it less healthy to eat. However, some forms of obesity are a result of genetic disorders and not diet. Nevertheless, what many people are concerned about is the recent increase in obesity rates, particularly in children, which I believe is partly a result of an increase in processed food consumption.

4 Refer students to the paragraph plan and elicit possible points for the development of the title.

Students write their own complete paragraphs and exchange them with a partner.

Using checklist questions 1–6, students check their partner's paragraph and discuss omissions or misunderstandings.

Refer students to Unit 4 Model answer, page 190. Ask them to underline the main idea of each paragraph and highlight the supporting ideas.

Listening p66

Section 4

Aim
Students improve comprehension by developing strategic approaches to listening.

1 Remind students that a systematic approach to listening can reduce nervousness and improve understanding.

Students reorder the exam strategies 1–7. Review as a class.

2 1.14 Students listen to the recording and answer questions 1–6. Answers are underlined in the recording script below.

Answers

1 (so-called) energy
2 herbal
3 not taking holidays
4 oxygen
5 caffeine
6 forgetful

1.14

Good morning. As part of our lecture series on everyday health issues, today's talk is on tiredness. We shall look at the main issues in turn, as well as some of the main research that has been carried out in this field.

Firstly it is clear that tiredness is on the rise. No official data exists on the rate of people reporting to doctors with recurring tiredness but it's a very common complaint. Research suggests that people are not relaxing properly and often work when they do not have enough energy. Furthermore, products to boost energy are also on the rise – sales of so-called energy drinks loaded with caffeine and sugar have grown by 23 per cent over the last year. And this is not the only instance of an increase in products claiming to boost energy. Guarana, a herbal stimulant, can now be found in everything from chocolate bars to tea bags.

Now let's examine what it is that's making people so tired. Dr Liebhold, a Sydney GP, has done extensive research into this and he believes that financial pressures, not taking holidays, and not having time off when you become ill due to fear of losing your job, are all common causes. Some of the other suggested causes are low oxygen levels in offices, poor diet, or illness. The problem is that tiredness is a symptom of just about every kind of illness which makes tracking down the cause all the more difficult.

The next question to ask is are people getting enough sleep? Dr Mansfield from Melbourne's Epworth Sleep Centre, who specializes in sleep disorders, says insomnia often arises when people are going through a stressful period. Mansfield often needs to re-educate people in how to get off to sleep. He recommends keeping your body clock regular by going to bed and rising at similar times every day, and not drinking too much caffeine. And there is some truth in the old story about having a glass of hot milk before bed. Milk contains the amino acid, tryptophan, which has been shown to help induce sleepiness.

Turning to the question of why we need sleep, researchers are still trying to answer this fundamental question. Sleep deprivation experiments have shown that after 14 days without sleep, rats will lie down and die. And after only three days' sleep loss, humans get confused, forgetful and start having hallucinations, so whatever sleep does, it is important.

Multiple choice

3 1.15 Students listen to the recording and answer questions 7 and 8. Answers are underlined in the recording script below.

Answers

7 C
8 B

1.15

Let's now look at the medical aspect of the problem. If on-going tiredness is present, a diagnosis of chronic fatigue syndrome might be considered. University of NSW expert, Professor Lloyd, says that by a process of elimination, researchers have tracked the site of this problem to the brain, and Lloyd believes it is a problem with the proper functioning of the brain, rather than any structural abnormality. The good news however is that most chronic fatigue sufferers make a full recovery within six months of being diagnosed.

The final area to examine is diet. Sydney-based naturopath Leonie McMahon, believes inadequate breakfast is a common cause of tiredness and recommends increasing the consumption of protein at breakfast.

Summary completion

4 1.16 Students listen to the recording and answer questions 9–12. Answers are underlined in the recording script below.

Answers

9 not convinced
10 energy levels
11 fatigue
12 whole grains

1.16

However, not all researchers feel the same way. Trent Watson, of the Dietitians Association, is not convinced by McMahon's theory explaining that our bodies don't really like to burn protein as a fuel so it doesn't really contribute to energy levels. Carbohydrates however, found in fruit, breads and pastas are a more common fuel. 'Anyone following a rigidly high-protein diet with low carbohydrates, even if they are operating at low intensity during the day, could subject themselves to fatigue because they just don't have the carbohydrate stores,' Watson says. In general, a good way to stay energized from a dietary point of view is to eat red meat, green leafy vegetables and whole grains. These foods give red blood cells the building blocks for optimum performance in their role of delivering oxygen to muscles.

To sum up, tiredness is a health problem on the increase and there continues to be much debate surrounding its causes and remedies. Now, if there are any questions I'd be happy to answer them.

Writing 2 p69

Task 2: Planning: Finding ideas 1

Aim
To develop students' writing by expanding on ideas and giving supporting points in the form of examples and explanations.

1 Explain that a perspective in writing is a specific point of view. Elicit examples of personal, local and international perspectives on health, nutrition and organic farming.

2 Students classify sentences 1–6 into personal, local/national, and global/international.

Answers

1 global/international
2 personal
3 local/national
4 global/international
5 local/national
6 personal

Further practice

Brainstorm personal, local and international ideas on *teenagers, middle-aged people* and *old-aged people*. Organize ideas in columns on the board. Identify main ideas and supporting points in brainstorming.

Students choose three ideas from the brainstorm and write a paragraph for each: one personal, one local and one international. They should extend and support their ideas with explanations or examples.

3 Students write paragraphs individually using the full range of ideas, explanations and examples collected from the discussion in Exercises 1 and 2.

Possible ideas

1 health – to avoid eating intensively farmed meat/fish
2 fashion – to emulate celebrity vegetarians
3 religion – maybe more people are turning to religions that advocate a vegetarian diet
4 environmental concern – maybe some people are becoming vegetarian out of concern for the environment (demand for meat leads to destruction of rainforest)
5 health – to follow a particular weight loss program

Argument/opinion questions 2: The opinion essay

Remind students that although they may be taking one side of the argument, they must still cover all the points in the essay title. Refer to the balanced argument approach in Unit 2, Writing, page 35.

5 Students discuss the question in pairs. Review as a class.

Answers

An opinion essay is perhaps most obvious but a balanced essay may also be successful if the student does not have strong views. If they adopt a balanced approach, students must make their own opinion clear throughout.

6

Answers

1 Yes.
2 Ask students to decide with a partner which are personal opinions and which refer to other people's opinions.

Some would argue that it would be better if food produce was not imported.

I firmly believe that this view is correct, and will discuss the reasons why in this essay.

It is certainly the case that importing food can have a negative effect on local culture.

Although some would argue that this is a natural part of economic development in an increasingly global world, I feel strongly that ...

Despite the fact that the trade in food exports has existed for many years, I am convinced that a reduction would bring significant financial and environmental gains.

In spite of this, the importance of developing local trade should not be undervalued.

In conclusion, I am certain that reducing food imports would have cultural and environmental benefits.

Refer students to the Useful language box on page 70, and point out the use of *it* as a subject of impersonal opinions. Ask students to decide which verbs they would use with personal opinions and which with impersonal or other people's opinions. (We would not usually use *assert, claim, confirm, insist, state* with personal opinions.)

Note: *I insist* is a very authoritarian way of expressing your wishes or opinion.

7

Answers

1 Other people
2 No strong opinion
3 agreeing with an idea
4 giving an opinion
5 Disagreeing with an idea
6 Other people

8 Students compare their arguments with those in Unit 4 Model answer, page 191.

Further practice

Refer students to Photocopiable 4, Exercise 3 (TB page 110).

Study skills p71

Planning: Finding ideas 2

Remind students that by adding a suffix we change the form of a word. For example by adding *-al* to the basic form of a word, we create an adjectival form.

1 Students complete the word formation and sentence completion exercises.

Answers

cultural, geographical, ecological, environmental, commercial, social

2

Answers

1 cultural
2 commercial
3 ecological/environmental
4 social

Further practice

For further practice in word formation, refer students to Photocopiable 4, Exercises 1 and 2 (TB page 110).

Dictionary focus p71

1

Students discuss the word forms and possible meanings of the words before checking in the dictionary and adding the words to their vocabulary bank.

5 The world we live in

Content overview

Themes

Natural disasters, natural processes, ecology and man's interaction with nature are the main themes of Unit 5. Students will read and write about natural and man-made processes and discuss problems associated with natural phenomena, endangered species and global warming.

Listening
- a radio programme about polar bears in Canada
- a lecture about cloning

Reading
- hurricanes

Writing
- natural and man-made processes

Exam related activities

Listening

Section 2 Flow chart completion
Short answers
Matching

Reading

Matching headings
Summary completion
Labelling a diagram
Short answer questions

Writing

Task 1 Describing:
- man-made processes
- natural processes

Speaking

Part 2 Describing and discussing animals and natural environments
Model answers
Part 3 Expanding on responses

Language development

Language focus

The passive
Discourse markers for ordering

Vocabulary

Adjectives and nouns

Skills development

Reading

Skimming for purpose and organization
Scanning for detail

Writing

Identifying and describing processes

Listening

Listening for detail

Pronunciation

Stressed syllables and schwa /ə/

Speaking

Discussing ideas and supporting opinions

Study skills

Register (formal / informal)

Dictionary focus

Academic Word List

Warm up p72

1 and 2 From the pictures, elicit vocabulary related to natural disasters and write it on the board. Vocabulary may include: *tsunami, tidal wave, earthquake, earth tremor, Richter scale, epicentre, aftershock, tornado, hurricane, whirlwind, typhoon, cyclone, monsoon, volcano, lava, eruption, crater, active/dormant, aid/government agencies.*

Ask students to compile a list of recent natural disasters and make notes of the results of these events. Students should then join another pair and describe the effects of the disasters. This should encourage students to use the passive.

Students note their opinions on who should be responsible for rescue and aid efforts, with specific examples, before joining a whole class discussion.

Reading p72

Aim
Readers of academic texts need to distinguish between the main ideas of a paragraph or an article and examples, supporting detail, and discussion. It is usually possible to establish the main purpose of a paragraph by examining the first sentence. The rest of the paragraph should provide explanation, exemplification or discussion of the main premise.

1

Answers

D

2 Before completing the exercise, ask students to underline / highlight the subject and main verb in the first sentence of each paragraph (reading passage, page 73) and decide on its purpose.

Answers

Para. A: *A hurricane is* (definition)
Para. B: *Hurricanes need* ... (causes of hurricanes)
Para. C: *Hurricanes produce* ... (effects of hurricanes)
Para. D: *Hurricanes are ... measured* (measurement of hurricanes)
Para. E: *... global warming is ... expected to produce* (effect of global warming)
Para. F: *All tropical storms are named* (identification of hurricanes)

Note: When checking the exercise, point out that in paragraph C the storm surge is discussed but is not the main point of the paragraph. Also, in paragraph E, the dates are a supporting detail.

Answers

1 i
2 v
3 vii
4 viii
5 iv

Further practice

Refer students to Photocopiable 5, Exercises 1 and 2 (TB page 111) for further practice in identifying the purpose of a text.

Summary completion

3 In pairs, students discuss whether the whole passage or part of it is being summarized (the whole passage is summarized).

Answers

6 tropics
7 category/strength
8 (many) buildings destroyed
9 global warming/climate change
10 male first names
11 meteorological region
12 (officially) retired

Labelling a diagram

Answers

13 cold air
14 eye/calm winds
15 spinning vortex (made up of high winds and heavy rainstorms)

Language focus p76

The passive

Aim
The passive voice is frequently used in scientific writing and formal research. In this section, students revise the forms and functions of the passive.

Explain that the passive is often associated with the description of artificial processes and when the event or the result is more important than the agent (the person or thing that causes the event). Elicit examples of artificial processes. Possibilities include: medical procedures, industrial production, construction, legislation and regulation, scientific experiments.

Revise the formation of the passive by referring students to Form in Unit 5 Grammar, page 173.

Ask students to underline examples of verbs in the passive in the reading passage and check their answers in pairs.

Para. A: *is called*

Para. B: *are formed, is sucked into, is named, is made up of*

Para. D: *are measured, was devised*

Para. E: *is expected*

Para. F: *are named, is being described, were named, are not used, have been retired*

1 Students complete the matching exercise.

Answers

1 d
2 e
3 c
4 b

2 Students discuss the answers to the questions in pairs.

Answers

1 The verbs in italics are all in the passive.
2 We form the passive using the verb *to be* + past participle.
3 1 present simple 2 present continuous 3 present perfect 4 modal passive
4 sentence 4 (by a country)

3

Answers

1 are heated
2 is heated
3 are given/have been given
4 is measured
5 was devised
6 is rated
7 is rated

Further practice

Refer students to the exercise in Unit 5 Grammar, page 174.

Now refer students to Photocopiable 5, Exercises 3 and 4 (TB page 112).

Vocabulary 1 p77

Adjectives and nouns

1 Review the functions of adjectives and remind students that in English adjectives come before nouns. Students work in pairs to discuss the questions.

Answers

a global, meteorological, structural, torrential, tropical, violent, active, disastrous
b catastrophic
c The *-al* ending is most common in news and academic writing.

2 In pairs, students complete the table.

Answers

-al: *central, national, normal, political*
-ent: *dependent, different, efficient, frequent*
-ive: *attractive, creative, effective, expensive*
-ous: *famous, religious, various*

3 Students complete the exercise individually and discuss their answers in pairs.

Answers

1 central
2 structural
3 violent
4 effective
5 various
6 religious/political
7 frequent
8 normal

Further practice

Refer students to Unit 5 Vocabulary, pages 181–182 for further practice of adjectives and nouns.

Students work in groups with large sheets of paper or OHTs to complete the table. Groups join each other and compare answers. Any misunderstandings can be clarified in a whole class discussion.

Listening 1 p77

Section 2

Aim
Students can improve their listening comprehension in lectures by reading, preparing questions on the lecture topic and discussing concepts in advance. By activating context-specific vocabulary and predicting lecture content, students can reduce the demands of listening for information and focus on the discursive elements of the lecture.

1 Students note their answers to the questions, discuss them with a partner and extend the discussion to a small group.

Flow chart

Students re-order the steps for completing flow charts individually and check their answers with a partner.

Answers

3, 2, 6, 4, 1, 5

2 1.17 Students listen and complete the flow chart to answer questions 1–4. Remind students to use no more than two words and / or a number for each answer. Answers are underlined in the recording script.

Answers

1 ashore
2 next six
3 migrate
4 seals

1.17

[A = Announcer; U = Usha]

A: This week's *Our World* programme comes from Canada where Usha Lee McFarling sends this report on how global warming is affecting the behaviour of polar bears and creating problems for the town of Churchill which depends on the bears for tourism.

U: The Hudson Bay polar bears are an unusual group. They spend half their year living on the frozen sea ice. And in a normal year, around springtime, when the weather gets warmer, the bears move ashore as the sea ice begins to melt. Once they have done this, their lives enter a new phase which involves a change in their metabolism. They don't hibernate, but their bodies slow down because they won't eat for the next six months. During this half of the year they lose hundreds of pounds in weight.

Each autumn, as the temperature falls, the bears migrate past the small town of Churchill waiting for the Hudson Bay to freeze over again. When it has, the bears go back onto the sea ice. Now they can build up their fat reserves by feeding on seals. They survive because the surface of the Hudson Bay is normally frozen from mid-October through to mid-April. During these months, the bears sleep on ice floes and swim in the frigid waters. Normally, that means million of dollars for the town of Churchill, which earns money by taking tourists into the tundra to see the bears as they pass by the town. However, recently the weather has been warmer and the bears' behaviour has changed. The warm weather prevents the sea from freezing and so the hungry bears come into town looking for food.

3 1.18 Students listen and answer questions 5–8. Remind them to check the instructions carefully. For these questions, students can answer using up to three words and / or a number. Answers are underlined in the recording script.

Answers

5 sleeping dart
6 (polar) bear prison
7 helicopter
8 natural (winter) habitat

1.18

Having spent six months without food, the bears are at their most hungry and dangerous. Starving bears often lose their natural wariness and wander into town. If a town resident spots a bear, they call the Bear Alert Programme on 679422 day or night, to report a bear in town. Officer Richard Romaniuk and his crew will then shoot the bear with a sleeping dart. It will then be taken to polar bear prison.

Sometimes the officers capture four bears in a day. To keep the animals from associating humans with food, they are not fed in prison. The bears are kept locked up until the sea freezes. Once the sea has frozen again the bears are airlifted by helicopter and flown back to return to their natural winter habitat.

The programme has two objectives. The first is to protect people from the bears. The second is to protect the bears from the people.

Short answers

4 1.19 Students listen and answer questions 9–14. Answers are underlined in the recording script.

Answers

9 $300 million
10 global warming
11 view bears
12 1,200
13 Northern Lights
14 *Snow Walker*

1.19

The town of Churchill has good reason to look after the bears. Rough estimates indicate the province of Manitoba earns in the region of $300 million each year from bear tourism. 'Bears are the backbone of our economy,' said town manager, Darren Ottaway.

While Ottaway is concerned about an abundance of hungry bears coming to town in the short term, he is even more worried that global warming may mean no bears here at all one day.

For three weeks during bear season, sleepy Churchill blooms as about 15,000 tourists stream through town hoping to get close-up views of the animals from caravans of heated Tundra Buggies. Several chartered jets unload bear-gazers at the Churchill airport each day. Hotels and restaurants closed during the bleak winter fill to capacity. Polar bears are not currently an endangered species. Their total population is estimated to be from 22,000 to 27,000. But the 1,200 Hudson Bay bears could face what scientists call a local extinction – they could produce fewer cubs and eventually die out.

Officials and business leaders in Churchill have already begun planning for alternative ways of generating income. Ottaway is promoting whale watching and is delighted that Japanese tourists are willing to brave the bone-chilling cold of winter to view the Northern Lights. 'It's super news for us,' Ottaway said of the potential Japanese tourist boom.

Warmer weather, Ottaway said, could also extend the shipping season on Hudson Bay and attract more filmmakers. The science-fiction classic *Iceman* was filmed nearby as well as an upcoming film, *The Snow Walker*. 'When people talk about climate change, you have to look at the benefits too,' Ottaway said.

Others, however, feel differently. 'The bears have been in our community for years,' said one resident. 'They're like neighbours and everybody ought to be helping to make sure their natural life cycle can be maintained.'

Pronunciation p80

The schwa sound /ə/

Explain that in fluent English conversation, speakers pronounce many consonants in unstressed syllables with the schwa sound, regardless of spelling.

1 and 2 1.20 Students underline the stressed syllables then listen to check their answers.

Students work in pairs listening to and correcting each other. Monitor this carefully as students may have difficulty distinguishing the stressed syllables.

Students listen a second (and third) time to identify syllables pronounced with schwa.

Repeat the practice and correction in pairs, focusing this time on the pronunciation of the schwa sound.

Answers

1.20

(schwa sounds are underlined)

1 ARea
2 CAtegory
3 comMUnity
4 eCOnomy
5 eNORmous
6 EStimate
7 MInor
8 pheNOmenon
9 poTENtial
10 REgion
11 REsident
12 STRategy

3 and 4 1.21 In pairs, students mark the stressed syllables and the schwa sounds in the sentences.

Play the recording. Pause after each sentence to give students a chance to check their answers.

Answers

1.21

(schwa sounds are underlined)

1 the HUDson BAY POlar BEARS are an unUsual GROUP.
2 SOMEtimes the OFficers CAPture FOUR BEARS in a DAY.
3 The TOWN of CHURchill has GOOD REAson to LOOK AFter the BEARS.
4 POlar BEARS are NOT CURrently an enDANgered SPEcies.
5 The BEARS have BEEN in our comMUnity for YEARS.

Speaking p80

1 Ask students to brainstorm vocabulary related to zoos and pets on a sheet of paper before interviewing each other. Vocabulary may include: *cages, enclosures, breeding programmes, free, wild, locked up, dangerous, extinct, domestic, tame, companionship, loyal, vet.*

2 Students answer the questions on the task cards in note form for both Part 2 topics before talking about them to a partner for one minute. Students check that their partner has answered all the prompt questions.

3 1.22 Prepare students to listen to the recording of a student answering one of these Part 2 questions. Ask them to answer the prompt questions as they listen.

Answers

a a camel
b large, has a hump
c visiting an uncle in a town where camel racing is popular
d move gracefully
e important national symbol

1.22

My favourite animal is a camel. It is quite a large animal and one thing about it that makes it easy to recognize is that it has a hump, either one or two, depending on the type. I think I saw my first camel when I went to visit my uncle. Er ... he lives in a town where camel racing is really popular so you see camels everywhere, sometimes just walking in the streets. I really like camels because, for me, they move so gracefully when they walk and I've always found it fascinating that they can survive for long periods without water. I feel the camel is an important symbol of my country because I guess many people associate camels with my country. Er ... it's also an important animal for food ... I mean we drink camel milk. And of course, racing camels make lots of money for their owners, so there's an economic aspect as well.

Aim
In Part 3 of the Speaking module, candidates are expected to answer questions about the background and current and future developments of a theme of general interest. They also need to give reasons for and justify their opinions. The ability to discuss ideas and support opinions with logical explanations and examples is practised in this section.

4 Ask students to write answers to the questions *Who? What? Where?* and *Why?* for 1, 2 and 3. Students then form groups of four to discuss and compare their suggestions. Refer them to the language of opinions in Unit 3, page 49.

5 1.23 Students listen to the recording and underline the expressions in the recording script on page 200 that answer the questions *Who? What? Where?* and *Why?* Answers are underlined in the recording script below.

Answers

Who? *governments/general public*
What? *laws/only buy dolphin-friendly tinned fish*
Where? *New Zealand and Australia*
Why? *dolphins could be in danger of becoming extinct*

1.23

Um ... I think there is a dual responsibility for protecting animals. Firstly, it is the responsibility of governments to make sure this happens. There should be laws to ensure, for example, that whales and dolphins are protected. I remember reading somewhere that quite a few dolphins get killed because they get caught in fishing nets. Of course, we, the general public, also have an important part to play in this. As far as dolphins are concerned, we can make sure we only buy tinned fish that is dolphin-friendly and what I mean by this is that the correct fishing methods have been used. I feel quite strongly that animals like dolphins must be protected because if we don't do this, dolphins could be in danger of becoming extinct and that would be a real shame. There would be other effects too, like to the tourist industry. Mmm ... I mean, if you think about it, in many countries, like New Zealand and Australia, tourists pay to go and look at the dolphins and even swim with them, which must be quite an unforgettable experience.

6 1.23 Explain that students can extend their answers by giving examples, causes and effects, and rephrasing. Ask if students recall any examples of expressions from the recording. Play the recording again for students to underline expressions in the recording script on page 200.

Answers are in underlined in the recording script below.

Answers

for example
as far as ... are concerned
what I mean by that is
because if we don't do this
like
I mean

1.23

I think there is a dual responsibility for protecting animals. Firstly, it is the responsibility of governments to make sure this happens. There should be laws to ensure, for example, that whales and dolphins are protected. I remember reading somewhere that quite a few dolphins get killed because they get caught in fishing nets. Of course, we, the general public, also have an important part to play in this. As far as dolphins are concerned, we can make sure we only buy tinned fish that is dolphin-friendly and what I mean by that is that the correct fishing methods have been used. I feel quite strongly that animals like dolphins must be protected because if we don't do this, dolphins could be in danger of becoming extinct and that would be a real shame. There would be other effects too, like to the tourist industry. I mean, if you think about it, in many countries, like New Zealand and Australia, tourists pay to go and look at the dolphins and even swim with them, which must be quite an unforgettable experience.

Listening 2 p82

Section 4

1 and 2 Elicit a definition of cloning, or read a dictionary definition and elicit the word. Brainstorm vocabulary related to cloning Vocabulary may include: *reproduction, identical, genetic, cell/stem cell, nuclear transfer, cell replacement, embryo splitting, ethics*. Ask students to discuss possible answers to 1–3.

3 1.24 Students write answers for questions 1–3.

Answers

1 His brother, Taz
2 Texas/in Texas/state of Texas/[in] a laboratory
3 [in] human transplants/transplant operations

1.24

Good morning and welcome to this series of lectures on man interfering with nature. This morning we are going to look at the issue of cloning. I'd like to begin by looking at some examples of animals that have been cloned before moving on to looking at how cloning is defined.

The first example I'd like to talk about is Idaho Gem, who was the very first mule to be cloned. Mules are a combination of horse and donkey. Idaho Gem is an identical copy of his brother, Taz, who is a racing champion, thus we can make the conclusion here that he was cloned to follow in his brother's footsteps. The next example I'd like to refer to is CC, which stands for CopyCat. Like her name suggests, she was the first cloned kitten. Interestingly, CC was created in a laboratory in the state of Texas by the very same scientists who made Dolly the sheep in Scotland. CC is physically identical to her mother, Rainbow, and what is important about this is that it has opened the doors for people to clone their pets in the future. Now the last animal example I'd like to look at today is the pig. In 2001, five piglets were born all female. They were created by a firm who claim that their birth is an important step for medicine. The idea is that pig organs and cells could be used in human transplants because the pigs have been cloned without a certain cell. This cell is a vital link because it is the one in human beings that is responsible for making the body reject donor organs. This means that not only is the transplant operation unsuccessful, but the patient's life could be at risk.

Now I'd like to discuss some of the current definitions of cloning.

Matching

4 1.25 Ask students to underline the keywords in questions 4–6.

Keywords are: 4 natural / identical copies / parent
5 produce / farm animals
6 embryo / laboratory / donor mother

Explain that keywords themselves may not always be on the recording, as they may be replaced with synonyms. Ask students to work in pairs to discuss possible synonyms for the following keywords: *identical* (*same type*), *farm animals* (*cattle*), *donor* (*foster*), *placed in* (*implanted*). Review with the whole class.

Answers

4 C
5 E
6 A

Explain that in this type of question, students will be asked to match an opinion with a statement on a scale of agreement or disagreement. Ask students to rate their own opinions about questions 7–10, using the same scale, before listening to the recording and answering the questions.

Answers

7 B
8 A
9 C
10 B

1.25 One kind of cloning, the kind commonly found in plants, occurs when plants reproduce themselves around the original plants known as the parent plants. New plants can then grow. This is quite a natural process by which plants can form more of the same type of plant.

Though you may not be aware of it, another type of cloning happens quite naturally in your body when old cells need to be replaced. Cells in your body split into two and make new chromosomes and it is the chromosomes that contain our genes. Embryo splitting is another form of cloning which can happen quite naturally when cells split to form two identical twins. You may then be asking yourself what all the fuss is about, if cloning does in fact happen naturally because sometimes man can interfere with nature and it can work. Take embryo splitting as an example. Now this type of cloning is quite common in farming and it is used to breed new bulls and cows. Embryos are placed into foster mother cows and these then grow into calves. And though some may consider this to be artificial, it has been going on for the last ten years with relatively few problems.

Now the last type of cloning I'd like to mention is perhaps the most controversial. This type of cloning is called nuclear transfer and it is when the nucleus of a cell is put into an egg of another animal that is genetically the same. This is done in a laboratory and after about five or six days, the embryo is implanted into a donor mother, which is how Dolly the sheep was made.

One argument in favour of cloning is that it can help in medicine as in the case of pigs being used in transplant operations. It is true that many people can wait for up to a year for a new kidney, and then still run the risk of their bodies rejecting the donor kidney; but will using pig organs really be the solution?

To answer this question, I'd like to take a look at some responses to the whole idea of using pig organs in humans. Neil Blackwood, who works for the company that cloned the five piglets, described it as a major medical advance that could solve the global problem of a lack of organs to use in transplant operations. This could lead in the future to saving human lives. Sheila Halliday, a leading transplant surgeon, does not share his view. She believes that although it is possible to use pig organs in humans, there are very real dangers. Halliday points out that diseases and infections could be passed from pig to human. Of course she does not yet know this for certain, which is why Halliday strongly advocates that more scientific research be done. She firmly believes pig organs should not be used in human operations until these findings are made public.

5 Ask students to make notes of their opinions on cloning with supporting reasons. Students must give three reasons for each of their opinions. Students discuss their opinions in pairs before joining another pair for a group discussion.

Writing p83

Task 1: Process diagrams 1

Aim

During their academic studies, students will be required to describe a range of processes which may include scientific experiments, social systems, historical developments and research methods. Students will need to be aware of the language of cause and effect, purpose and systematization.

1 Explain that processes may be linear (a production line), cyclical (a life cycle), systematic (an information flow chart), natural or man-made.

Explain that diagrams may be pictorial or non-pictorial.

Answers

Diagram A – linear process, non-pictorial, man-made

Diagram B – cyclical process, natural, pictorial

Students make notes of two further examples of processes and classify them as cyclical / linear / systematic / natural / man-made. Ask students to suggest the most effective diagrams to depict the processes they have suggested and to draw the diagrams on large sheets of paper or OHTs to show to the rest of the group in Exercise 4.

2 Students match the descriptions in sentences i and ii to Diagrams A and B. Point out that factual processes are described in the present tense. When the process is natural, the verb will be in the active voice. The passive voice is used for man-made processes.

Students underline the verbs in sentences i and ii and discuss in pairs which tense they are in and why.

Answers

Diagram A – ii

Diagram B – i

(Questions 1 and 2)

i the present simple active is used to describe natural processes (*enlarges/becomes/appear*)

ii the present simple passive is used to describe a man-made process (*is inspected/are met/can be furnished/must be decorated*).

3 Students complete the sentences in pairs and check their answers in small groups.

Answers

1 different
2 purpose
3 order
4 changed
5 passive
6 active
7 present

4 Elicit responses from the whole class.

Suggested answers

a) sending a text message
b) paper recycling
c) the water cycle
d) how bees make honey

Students show the diagrams they have prepared in Exercise 1 to the class and explain the processes.

5 Using the example of the water cycle, elicit the vocabulary for presenting the steps in a process in the correct order. Possible suggestions are: *first, then, after, finally, when*.

Answers

1 The step after this
2 Gradually,/Over time,
3 At this point in the cycle,
4 in order to
5 Gradually,/Over time,
6 As a result of
7 The final stage of the cycle is when
8 Having completed all these steps

6

Suggested answers

(Question 2)
0 To begin with,
1 The next stage of the cycle,
2 Eventually,
3 At the same time,
4 so as to

7 Ask students to find *nectar, pollen* and *pollinate* in a dictionary and discuss the definitions with a partner.

Students order the steps of the process before referring to Exercise 2 to decide which tense and voice to use in their paragraph (natural process = present tense / active voice). Refer students to the Grammar section of Unit 4, pages 172–173 for revision of relative clauses.

Students write paragraphs individually and compare them with copies of the model answer below.

Model answer

To begin with, the bee searches for suitable flowers. Eventually, the bee finds a flower and extracts nectar, which it needs in order to make honey. At the same time, pollen from the flower sticks to the bee's legs. The final stage of the process is when the bee finds another flower and repeats the process, which helps pollinate the flower.

8 Ask students to identify the cause, effect or purpose in each sentence before rewriting them. Point out that students will need to change word forms as well as vocabulary.

Answers

(discuss grammatically correct alternatives)
1 Apples are carefully packed in boxes in order to stop them bruising.
2 Yeast is mixed into the bread dough so that the bread rises.
3 As a result of a drop in the ocean floor, a tsunami wave is produced.
4 The temperature drops below zero degrees, which results in snowflakes forming.

9 Refer students to the model answer 'A straw bale house construction', page 191 and ask them to underline all the words that have been taken from the diagram on page 83 and changed. Review word forms with the whole class.

Answers

1 prepared (v) – preparation (n)
installation (n) – installed (v)
electrics (n) – electrical (adj)
insulation (n) – insulated (v)
inspection (n) – inspected (v)
decoration (n) – decorated (v) – decorative (adj)
carpet (n) – carpeting (n)
furnishing (n) – furnished (v)
2 are positioned and secured/is installed/is completed/ is insulated/is inspected/are met/be furnished/be decorated/is finished

Further practice

10 Students use the paragraph plan and the Useful language box, page 85, to write the Task 1 essay and exchange their work with a partner. In pairs, students highlight or underline the following elements of the essay: starting point of process / first half of process / purpose / result of main stages / second half of process / result of process / finished or cyclical.

Refer students to the model answer 'The carbon cycle', page 191, and ask them to underline all the words that refer to the process and compare them with their own use of process vocabulary.

Answers

goes through as it
To begin with,
After this stage,
As a result of
The final stage

Study skills p87

Academic vocabulary

Aim
Students will need to follow the conventions of formality or register in academic writing. Register is reflected in the use of technical or Latinate vocabulary (not phrasal verbs), impersonal opinions and the passive voice.

1 Students match the alternatives.

Answers

1 D
2 G
3 A
4 F
5 C
6 H
7 E
8 B

2

Answers

Noun	Verb	Adjective	Adverb
analysis	analyse	analysed	
environment	–	environmental	environmentally
data	–	–	–
indicator	indicate	indicative	–
evidence	(evidence)	evidential	(evidently)
climate	–	climatic	–
source	source	–	–
creator	create	creative	creatively
policy	–	political	politically
requirement	require	required	–
individual	(individualize)	individual	individually
procedure	proceed	procedural	–
majority	(major)	major	–
research researcher	research	–	–
–	identify	identifiable identified	identifiably
significance	signify	significant	significantly
benefits	benefit	beneficial	(beneficially)
legislation	legislate	legislative	(legislatively)
finance	finance	financial	financially
economy	economize	economic economical	economically

Dictionary focus p87

Explain that the Academic Word List (AWL) was designed to help students prepare for university study and is based on the frequency of written words in the Academic Corpus. The AWL excludes the 2,000 words in the General Service List (GSL) which was created by Michael West in 1953 and contains the words of most use to learners of English. Students need to have knowledge of this before studying the AWL. Refer students to John Bauman's site for information on the GSL (www.jbauman.com).

Students check the meanings of the words in the dictionary and add them to their vocabulary bank. They can then look for the words on the AWL and GSL.

6 Going places

Content overview

Themes

Unit 6 focuses on the themes of travel and tourism, including student travel, transport systems, the cultural, economic and ecological effects of tourism. Students will read about and discuss these themes from a local and personal perspective.

Listening
- a dialogue about low cost travel for students
- a lecture on transport, geography and economics

Reading
- tourism and innovation
- tourism and culture

Writing
- organizing and writing problem/solution essays

Exam related activities

Listening

Section 1 Short answers
YES/NO
Multiple choice

Section 4 Table completion
Summary completion

Reading

Multiple choice
Map completion
Sentence completion

Writing

Task 2 Problem/solution essays

Speaking

Part 2 Discussing the advantages and disadvantages of different forms of transport

Part 3 Discussing travel and tourism in the past, present and the future

Language development

Language focus

Reference and substitution
Conditionals (1st, 2nd)
Modality (expressing possibility and probability)

Vocabulary

Lexical cohesion for:
- cause/effect
- problem/solution

Synonyms

Skills development

Reading

Scanning for opinions
Finding parallel expressions

Writing

Planning and writing introductions
Paraphrasing
Organizing and writing essays

Listening

Listening for detail

Study skills

Revising and editing your writing

Dictionary focus

Parts of speech

Warm up p88

Introduce the topic of holidays by referring students to the photo. Elicit holiday and transport related vocabulary by asking general questions such as: *Where are they taking their holiday? How do you think they got there?*

Refer students to the pictures of modes of transport (ferry, plane and hovercraft) on page 89. Discuss whether these modes of transport are common in students' home countries.

Ask students to write brief answers to 1–3.

Students compare their answers in pairs, note the differences and report back to the class.

Listening 1 p88

Section 1

Aim
Many UK students take *a gap year* (a year away from studying, often spent travelling) between leaving school and starting university. They also travel, as cheaply as possible, during the long university vacations. *Railcards* and *youth travel cards* are both means of getting discounts on fares and *youth hostels* offer simple shared accommodation at low prices. This section practices the language needed to compare different means of travel, discuss the costing and make bookings.

1 1.26 Explain the different types of answer required.

For questions 1–2, students must write short answers. They must limit their answers to two words and / or a number.

For questions 3–6, students must answer A or B. Students must be careful to write A or B, not RECOMMEND / DOES NOT RECOMMEND.

Give students time to read the questions before they listen. Play the recording and ask students to answer questions 1–6 only. Students compare their answers in pairs and discuss differences. Answers are underlined in the recording script.

Answers

1 France/In France
2 £1,100
3 A
4 B
5 A
6 B

1.26

[TA = Travel agent; S = Student]

TA: Good morning. How can I help you?

S: I'm thinking of taking a year off university next year and I'd like to travel around Europe.

TA: OK then. Do you have any idea where you'd like to go?

S: Well, I was thinking of starting in France and then working my way up to Eastern Europe, possibly going as far as Slovakia.

TA: Well, there are a number of ways you can do this and we have various options available. It really depends on your budget and how you'd like to travel.

S: That's just the thing really. Um ... I mean I've just finished my second year at university so obviously I'd like to do it in as cheap a way as possible.

TA: That's fine. Could you give me a rough idea of the price range you're looking at?

S: Realistically speaking, I'm hoping to pay between about £700 and £900. I could stretch to £1,100, but that's really my limit.

TA: How long are you thinking of going for?

S: About ten months.

TA: To be honest, you'd be better off travelling for about seven months if that's your budget.

S: OK, that's not too bad. So how would you suggest I travel?

TA: Well, because of the time limit, I don't think walking is a viable option. Of course in this day and age, the most convenient way to get around is by flying, particularly if you've got quite a bit you want to see in a short space of time. Saying that, I still think the best way to get around Europe is by train. As a student, you can also get a student railcard, which means cheaper fares.

S: That sounds brilliant. How do I go about getting a railcard?

TA: Well, if you decide that's what you want to do, then we can organize that all for you. You'll need to fill in a form and provide us with two passport photos and we'll do the rest. It costs about £36 plus about £10 administration costs.

S: Great, that's really not expensive at all. And what about buses? I was just thinking if I decide to go to places which are a bit more remote.

TA: There are always local buses, but these are not always a good idea. They can be quite unreliable and in some areas quite dangerous because the buses tend to be overcrowded and some of the drivers drive way too fast. So I would suggest you don't do this.

S: That sounds quite frightening! So what are my options then?

TA: You could hire a car, but it can be expensive. Still I do think if you're thinking about going to smaller towns and places which are off the beaten track, then hiring a car is by far the better way to do it. You can also look at sharing the costs by hiring a car with someone else.

S: That's a good idea. I guess I could put a message on the Internet.

TA: You could do that, but don't forget that you meet people when you're travelling and you'll probably find someone who's going to the same place as you are.

S: That's true. I want to stay in youth hostels so I'm sure I'll find people who are interested in going to the same places. One last thing, what about taxis? I was thinking about if I go out at night. I use taxis all the time here.

TA: Ah, but taxis abroad are a different story. In certain countries, they're no problem, but by and large, taxi fares are high. If you do go out at night try walking home, but make sure you don't do this alone. Try and find people to go out with at night or come home at a reasonable time. But if you're staying in youth hostels, you should find plenty of young people to go out with at night.

S: I'm sure I will.

2 1.27 For questions 7–9, students must choose one of the options A, B or C (multiple choice). Explain that multiple-choice questions sometimes contain false clues or distracters and that it is important to read the questions very carefully.

Possible distracters for 7–9 are:

7 A (a ferry ticket is usually the cheapest option)

8 A (I don't have my cheque book with me)

9 C (a later flight at 11.30)

Play the recording for students to answer questions 7–9.

Students compare answers in pairs and discuss differences.

Answers

7 B
8 C
9 B

Review the answers with the whole class and play the recording a second time to give students a chance to listen again and check.

1.27

[TA = Travel agent; S = Student]

TA: Now have you thought about how you'd like to travel to France?

S: Not really, no.

TA: There are basically three ways you can go, by ferry which leaves every day and night, or there's the hovercraft which is more pricey, but will get you there quicker and, of course, you could fly.

S: Well, I don't think flying is an option for me as it'll be too expensive so I suppose I'll choose one of the other two. It's a pity really as I don't fancy the idea of travelling by sea. Last time I did that, I got terribly seasick.

TA: Well, you're in luck then as at the moment there's a special deal on flights to France. In fact a plane ticket is now half the price of a ferry ticket which is usually the cheapest option.

S: That's great, I'll do that then. I much prefer flying anyway.

TA: I'll need to get some details off you then. Firstly, how will you be paying – cash, cheque or credit card? If you pay by cheque, you'll need a cheque guarantee card.

S: I don't have my cheque book with me so it'll have to be by credit card.

TA: Fine, that's no problem. If you could just sign over here, and then we'll have look at flight times and I can sort out a youth travel card for you.

S: Fine. Can I use your pen, please?

TA: No problem. Now let's look at times. There is flight leaving at 9.00 a.m. and one that leaves half an hour later. Or you can choose a later flight at 11.30.

S: No, I think 11.30 is too late so I think I'd prefer the flight that leaves after 9.00. I'm not very good at getting up in the morning!

TA: No problem, just give me a moment. Right, that's booked for you. Please remember that if you want to change this, you must give 24 hours notice or you will lose your place.

3 Ask students to make notes on the advantages and disadvantages of travelling before or after studying at university. Students then form groups to discuss their ideas.

Listening 2 p90

Section 4

Aim

The language and the structure of lectures is more formal than that of dialogues and conversations. A formal speaker will announce the topic of the talk at the beginning of the lecture and give the listeners an outline of the key areas of discussion. He/She will use signposting language to indicate transitions from one part of the talk to another.

1 1.28 Explain that the lecture students will hear is about the relationship between the geographical features of several countries and the forms of transport most commonly used in each. Indicate Colombia, Venezuela, the UK, Belgium, China and Japan on a world map and elicit vocabulary for geographical features and transport. Vocabulary includes: *mountains, forests, highlands, inland waterways, canals, steamers, ships, domestic flights, road networks, rail system, seaports*.

Emphasize that for questions 1–6, students must limit their answers to two words and / or a number.

Play the recording and ask students to answer questions 1–6. Answers are underlined in the recording script.

Students compare their answers in pairs and discuss differences.

Answers

1 commercial airline
2 400
3 Highlands/the Highlands
4 4,000 km
5 17%
6 90%

1.28

Good morning and welcome to this morning's lecture on transport. What I'll be doing today is comparing forms of transport in different countries to see how forms of transport are affected by factors such as geographical landscape and economic development. My focus will be on countries in South America, Europe and Asia.

The first country I'd like to look at is Colombia, which is in South America. This is a country where geography plays an important role. Due to the huge amount of mountains and forests in this country, travelling by air is crucial. I don't know if many of you realize this fact, but Colombia was the first country to establish a commercial airline and in so doing they made aviation history. Today there are more than 400 airports in Colombia for domestic flights which highlights the point I made earlier that air travel is a vital means of transport in this country. Colombia also has a road network of about 48,000 km linking Colombia to Venezuela and Ecuador. Transport by road is important for trade as well as tourism. Apart form this, there is also a railway system, but it is in need of modernization. The other means of transport is by steamers with the *Magdalena* being the main waterway. Now let's turn to Colombia's neighbour, Venezuela. Once again we see that internal flights are an important means of transport as, like Colombia, Venezuela has remote areas where flying is the easiest means of travelling from A to B. Trains are not popular and most of the railway lines are in the Highlands as this is where the iron ore mines are. Trains are an efficient means of transporting the iron ore from the mines to the factories thus we can see how transport and the economy are inter-related. Ships are also used extensively in this country and there are many ports, the main seaports being Puerto Cabello and Guanta.

Turning now to Europe. Belgium is a country that boasts one of the most compact railway systems worldwide. This is possibly unsurprising in a country that is highly industrialized and a major European export country. Just under half of all that Belgium produces is manufactured for export. Inland waterways, or canals, are also an important means of transport, transporting both freight and people. Belgium also has the third largest seaport in the world, namely Antwerpen. Air travel is also important, although this is not linked to geographical terrain, as is the case in the South American countries we've already looked at.

Next I'd like to look at the United Kingdom. Like Belgium, the UK has inland waterways, around 4,000 km, yet only about 17% of these are used for commercial transport. The main inland port is Manchester and the chief seaport is London with Southampton taking second place. Air travel is extensive in this country and there are around 150 airports, the most famous being Heathrow. However, about 90% of passengers in the UK travel by road.

2 1.29 Emphasize that for questions 7–12 students must limit their answers to a maximum of three words or a number.

Play the recording and ask students to answer questions 7–12. Answers are underlined in the recording script.

Students compare their answers in pairs and discuss differences.

Answers

7 geographical size/geography
8 two levels/tiers
9 trains
10 250 km
11 international
12 domestic

1.29

Finally, I'd like to look at two Asian countries. China is a country which reveals how geographical size affects transport development. Roads and railways are widely used and this has led to a huge amount of bridges being built such as the Yangtse Bridge which is probably the most widely known. The Yangtse Bridge is 1.6 km long and is built on two levels. The upper tier is for cars and pedestrians while the lower is for trains. Railways are especially important and over 80% of freight and passengers are transported by rail. With such a high proportion of people using trains, it is not surprising that governments in countries like China are prepared to invest in the railway system. Obviously, a fast and effective train service will encourage businesses and the general public to continue using it. The last country I'm going to mention is Japan which has one of the most advanced transport systems in the world. The railway system is highly developed and the Tokaido railway, connecting Tokyo and Osaka has trains that can travel up to 250 km per hour. Ships are also a vital means of transport, in both international and domestic areas.

To summarize, we can see that transport varies throughout the world, yet the importance of transport networks, be they air, sea, rail or road cannot be underestimated.

Further practice

Refer students to Photocopiable 6, Exercise 1 (TB page 113) and play the recording again for them to note the signposting language.

Reading p90

Recognizing opinions in a passage

Aim

In this section, students practise identifying writers' opinions and the purpose of the reading passage.

1 Elicit typical problems experienced by small villages, for example limited employment opportunities, a declining permanent population, an ageing population.

Ask students to read the title of the passage and to discuss what they think the problem in this village may be. What do they think the solution may be?

This is an opportunity to highlight the use of modals to express probability. Refer students to the Useful language box on page 101 for the use of *might, may, could* for speculating.

Ask students to read the passage carefully and then answer questions 1 and 2.

Answers

1 No.
2 A

Multiple-choice questions

2 Ask students to read questions 1 and 2 carefully. Then ask them to look for the answers in the reading passage.

Answers

1 C
2 C

Completing a map

3

Answers

3 Kramsach
4 mirrors/heliostats/reflectors
5 fort

Sentence completion (no list)

4 Explain that some of the answers to the questions in the exam will be the same as the words used in the text, but sometimes students will need to find parallel or similar expressions. The questions follow the order of the text.

Refer students to the italicized words in questions 6–12 and ask them to highlight the parallel expressions in the text.

Answers

6 driving away (lines 18–19)
7 built its reputation and wealth on (line 29)
8 reflect the light accurately (line 40)
9 one in five, syndrome (lines 79 and 82)
10 has fallen (lines 104–105)
11 blind (line 119)
12 plan to shut down (line 146)

5

Answers

6 tourists and inhabitants
7 crystal glass production
8 completely flat/precision-engineered
9 SAD/Seasonal Affective Disorder
10 permanent population
11 motorists
12 regional court house

Matching: People and opinions

6 Review the rule that, in English, proper nouns (the names of people, places, months of the year and organizations) start with capital letters, and explain that this makes them easier to find in the text.

Students complete questions 13–18 individually and check their answers with their partners.

Answers

13 C
14, 15 A, C
16 D
17, 18 A, B

Further practice

Refer students to Photocopiable 6, Exercise 2 (TB page 113) to practise scanning for names.

Understanding reference and substitution

Aim
This section focuses on the use of referents to avoid repetition and increase cohesion in written texts.

Elicit examples of personal pronouns such as *he, she, it, they, one,* demonstrative pronouns such as *this, that* and *these,* relative pronouns such as *which* and *that.* Explain the use of these pronouns to replace nouns and ask students to write examples on the board.

1 Students work in pairs to find the pronouns in the reading passage on page 91 and their referents.

Answers

1 the sun
2 Rattenberg's
3 mirrors
4 sunshine
5 SAD and/or the syndrome created by a shortage of light
6 (the people of) the village
7 concerns
8 Dr Peter Erhard

2

Answers

1 a force of nature
2 a sun
3 bathe the entire village in light
4 the imagination

If students find Exercise 2 difficult, help them to rewrite the sentences so that they do not contain the expressions in Exercise 2. Make sure that students understand this form is not acceptable. For example

*But just as the obstacle that blights Rattenberg is **a force of nature, a force of nature** too is the solution …*

3 Students compare their answers in pairs.

Suggested answers

1 did so
2 one
3 it
4 do so
5 that
6 so
7 those
8 its
9 it

Vocabulary p95

Lexical cohesion

Introduce the lexical categories to be studied: *problem, solution, cause, effect, action/activity, quantity, argument.* Write them in columns on the board and elicit relevant vocabulary.

1 Ask students to use a dictionary to organize the words into categories. Examples from the text are already given.

Answers

1 solution/effect: result, alternative, consequence, outcome
2 action/activity: project, scheme
3 size/quantity: number, amount, extent, scope
4 argument/opinion: controversy, discussion, debate, viewpoint, dispute, answer, event

2 Ask students to complete the text with words from Exercise 1.

Students compare answers and discuss discrepancies.

Answers

1 numbers
2 solution
3 activity
4 moves/actions
5 effects/consequences
6 argument
7 result/effect/consequence
8 extent
9 alternatives/solutions

Further practice

Students complete the sentences in Unit 6 Vocabulary, page 182.

Language focus p96

Conditional sentences

Real conditionals

Explain that first or real conditionals are used to express possible and probable results or solutions to problems.

1 Explain that *provided (that), supposing (that)* and *as/so long as* can replace *if*.

Unless introduces a negative condition (*if not*) which affects the verb in the second clause. For example *If the people of Rattenberg do not obtain funding, they will go bankrupt.*

Elicit examples of *unless* from students' daily life to reinforce the difference between *unless* and the other conditionals.

Answers

1 Problem: possible bankruptcy/cost of the mirrors
Solution: EU funding
2 ***Unless*** *the people of Rattenberg obtain European Union funding, they will/may/might/could become bankrupt.*
Provided (that)/Supposing (that)/As long as *the people of Rattenberg obtain European Union funding, they will/may/might/could be saved from bankruptcy.*

2 Ask students to write solutions to problems 1–4 and discuss them in small groups.

Unreal conditionals

1 Review sentence a as an example of second conditional forms, explaining that second conditionals express possibility, but not probability.

a If Hawaii *banned* tourism, the economy *would/may/might/could be* badly *affected*.

(It is **possible** for Hawaii to ban tourism, but **not at all probable** because it depends on tourism for a large part of its income.)

Practise and reinforce the use of past tense + would by eliciting examples of possible but unlikely events from students' daily lives.

Question 1. In pairs, students identify the tenses and discuss the functions of the conditionals.

Answers

1 b
2 a
3 c

Question 2. Individually, students write answers to 1–5. They then form groups and use their answers to discuss each question.

Go through possible answers with the whole class.

Suggested answers

1 If there were congestion charges for all privately-owed vehicles entering city centres, more people would be encouraged to use public transport.
2 If penalties were placed on the use of private cars, this would be unfair to people living in areas which are poorly served by public transport.
3 If laws to discourage the use of private transport had been introduced earlier, our cities would not be so polluted.
4 If taxes on petrol had been increased, the money could have been invested in public transport.
5 If politicians worried less about winning votes, they might do more to address the problem of pollution in cities.

Further practice

For further practice of conditionals, ask students to complete the exercise in Unit 6 Grammar, page 175.

Writing 1 p97

Task 2: Understanding introductions

Aim
The introduction can be described as the map of the essay. Firstly, it guides the writer, and secondly it indicates to the reader what to expect in the main body of the essay. The introduction should include:

- the topics that are going to be covered
- the focus
- the writer's point of view
- how the writer intends to present the essay

1 Students establish the topic and the task by answering 1 and 2.

<u>Private car ownership</u> (topic) has grown dramatically in recent years. This has led to a rise in <u>traffic congestion.</u> (topic) <u>What could governments and individuals do</u> to reduce congestion? (task)

Answers

1 Traffic congestion due to car ownership.
2 To suggest possible solutions by governments and individuals.

2 Ask students to distinguish the topic (traffic congestion) from the specific aspect of the topic (the contribution of private car ownership to congestion) and to state their opinion on the responsibility of governments and individuals for traffic congestion. Students highlight or underline the words in the example introduction that state the writer's intention (*outline* and *evaluate*).

Answers

1 Sentence 2 states the writer's opinion, Sentence 3 explains the focus of the essay
2 Yes, although giving your opinion is optional unless specifically asked for (see Unit 4).

Paraphrasing the question

3 Students work in pairs to find paraphrases in the model introduction on page 97.

Answers

ownership = *own car*

grown = *growing*

a rise = *an increase*

to reduce = *reducing*

4

Answers

1 answer
2 problem
3 belief
4 worry
5 significant
6 explain
7 improve
8 view
9 affect

5 Introduce examples of the gerund as a subject, for example:

Avoiding *traffic jams is one advantage of travel by train.*

Travelling *by train is one way of reducing traffic congestion.*

Suggested answers

1 Solving the issue of sound pollution from planes is difficult.
2 The importance of encouraging types of transport that are friendly to the environment is a priority for people in government.
3 Transporting goods by rail is less environmentally damaging.
4 Rising oil costs are causing anxiety.
5 Reducing energy waste should be the first aim of a government.

Writing introductions

Aim
In this section, students practise expanding on main ideas by including examples.

6 Students refer to the Useful language box on page 99 to expand parts 1, 2 and 3 of the introductory paragraph. Students then compare their answers with a partner.

Students identify phrases which introduce ideas, explain focus, give opinions, outline arguments and counter arguments, and identify the task.

Answers

Unit 2: Sentence 1 = In modern society, Sentence 2 = The issue is, Sentence 3 = The arguments ... need to be examined.
Unit 4: Sentence 1 = recent advances, Sentence 2 = While this development, Sentence 3 = I partly agree, Sentence 4 = This essay will
Unit 8: Sentence 1 = The issue of, Sentence 2 = Some argue, Sentence 3 Others feel, Sentence 4 = This essay will
Unit 10: Sentence 1 = There are different views, Sentence 2 = Some argue that ... whilst others point to, Sentence 3 = It is my belief

7 Students write paragraphs for questions 1 and 2 and exchange them with a partner. Students underline the phrases in their partner's paragraphs that introduce the main parts of the introduction and discuss any omissions or errors.

Speaking p99

1 Elicit and discuss vocabulary for different forms of transport in other countries. Identify more / less popular forms of transport and ask students to give explanations for their relative popularity or unpopularity.

Answers

Public transport: commuter/train/bus/fare/tram/taxi

Private transport: bicycle/car/tollbooth/motorway/motorcycle

2 In Part 2, candidates are expected to talk for 1–2 minutes on a set topic. They are given four questions to guide their talk. By answering these questions, students can develop their topic coherently. Students can make their talk more interesting and show their language ability by including descriptions and giving examples.

3 Make sure that students are preparing their talk by writing the answers to the questions on the topic card and that they are timing each other (they should have one minute to prepare).

Check that Student B is making notes while Student A is speaking (and vice versa), and that the talk is timed (1–2 minutes).

Give students time to convert their notes into questions before they check with each other.

4

> **Aim**
> In Part 3 of the IELTS Speaking module, students are expected to discuss, compare, suggest, speculate and give opinions on topics of general interest.

Ask students to make brief notes on questions 1–6 before forming groups and discussing each question.

Writing 2 p100

Task 2: Problem and solution questions

1

Answers

Unit 2 tasks = discuss arguments for/against
Unit 4 tasks = give your own view
Unit 6 tasks = describe solutions to a problem

2 Students find synonyms in the paragraph for *problem* and *solution*.

Answers

1 problem = *issue, drawback*
  solution = *proposal*
2 It is used to express possibility or hypothetical situations rather than certainty.

3

> **Aim**
> Problem/solution essays not only include suggestions for ways to resolve difficulties, but also require an evaluation of the solution. This may take the form of a counter-argument (or refutation), suggesting alternative possibilities and speculating on the results.

After working in pairs to develop arguments and counter-arguments, students form small groups to develop a discussion of one or two of the problems.

4

Suggested answers

1 a large number of
2 many people believe, often
3 would probably
4 certain, is highly likely to be
5 certain, the majority of accidents involve

Refer students to Unit 9, pages 140–141 for detailed practice of modals.

5 Students plan paragraphs for three of the problems in Exercise 3, page 101. Students exchange their paragraphs with a partner who should check that the paragraphs include:

- a solution
- advantages
- disadvantages
- an evaluation of the advantages and disadvantages

6 In pairs, students generate ideas from the mind map before using the paragraph plan to organize their ideas for a Task 2 essay. Students write the essay individually.

7 Students compare their essay with the model answer on page 192. Students should underline topic sentences at the beginning of each paragraph, problems, solutions and evaluations of the consequences.

Study skills p103

Editing 1: Editing your writing

1 and 2 Students work in pairs to match the grammar mistakes to the examples and write the correct sentences.

Answers

1 F Relaxing visa regulations would be fairer for overseas students, particularly as their tuition fees *are* normally much higher than those for home students.
2 A Playing computer games, a common pastime for young people, is fast becoming a major cause of poor social skills.
3 B Tourism is a much-needed source of income in developing *countries*.
4 C It is undeniable that *young children* are easily attracted by advertising campaigns.
5 E Older people are more reluctant to travel long-distances because *they* are less prepared to take risks.

6 H (accept any reasonable answer) These two charts are clear examples that different climate conditions in European countries vary considerably.
7 I In other words, their daily lives also include elements of traditional culture such as language, food and fashion.
8 G On the *other* hand, other groups argue that it is the *responsibility* of governments to maintain roads.
9 D This suggests *having* a fast and efficient train system will encourage the general public to *use* private transport less.

Dictionary focus p103

Individually, students find the words in the dictionary and make a note of the parts of speech. In pairs, they discuss their answers.

Refer students to Photocopiable 6, Exercise 3 (TB page 114) for practice in deducing the meaning of words from their context.

7 The world of work

Content overview

Themes

Unit 7 focuses on international trade and the effect of globalization on local agriculture. It discusses employment, the effects of stress at work and employment issues for people with disabilities.

Listening
- a talk about temporary employment for people with special needs

Reading
- a newspaper article about McDonald's
- an article about work overload

Writing
- interpreting graphs and diagrams about work and industry

Exam related activities

Listening

Section 2 Sentence completion
Short answers
Table completion

Reading

True / False questions
Flow chart completion
Short answer questions
Note completion

Writing

Task 1 Multiple diagrams

Speaking

Predicting the future
Expressing certainty / uncertainty

Language development

Language focus

Clauses introduced by *that*
Complex sentence structures

Vocabulary

Synonyms for people

Skills development

Reading

Prediction
Scanning for detail
Scanning for opinion

Writing

Describing data in diagrams

Listening

Prediction
Listening for detail

Pronunciation

Linking

Study skills

Editing written work

Dictionary focus

Collocations

Warm up p104

Elicit the names of multinationals and ask students which of these is most popular / common in their country. Do any multinationals have different names in other countries (for example Wal-Mart in the USA is Asda in the UK)? Which are the largest multinationals? (Wal-Mart, BP, ExxonMobil, Shell, General Motors)

1 and 2 Students note their answers to the questions before discussing them with a partner. Pairs then join together to form small groups for further discussion.

Reading 1 p104

Aim
By predicting the possible content and viewpoint of articles and reports, students can activate their prior knowledge of topics and prepare ideas for written and spoken discussion. This helps to prepare students for lectures, essays and seminar discussions. Titles, subtitles, diagrams, tables and article abstracts are all useful pointers to the content of the text and the writer's attitude.

1 Once students have discussed the questions in pairs, they can contribute to a plenary discussion.

Some facts about McDonald's (taken from the website www.mcdonalds.com).

- McDonald's has more than 30,000 restaurants worldwide.
- McDonald's restaurants serve more than 50 million people in 119 countries daily.
- McDonald's was founded by Ray Croc.
- McDonald's opened its first restaurant in Des Plaines, Illinois in 1955. The first day's revenue was $366.12.
- Ronald McDonald's first television appearance was in 1963.
- The Big Mac was introduced in 1968 and the Egg McMuffin was introduced in 1973.

2 and 3 Students underline keywords in the title that may answer questions 1 and 2 (*fruit*/ *Big Mac*/*so much ... that* = cause and effect). The first sentence confirms that apples are the fruit in question.

Answers

1 B
2 C

True, False, Not Given

Ask students to find examples in the reading text of the words in 1–5 on page 106 and underline them. Students check answers in pairs.

4

Answers

1 False (*will soon be joined by*)
2 True (*No one knows whether*)
3 Not Given
4 False (*have not had a comparable influence*)
5 False (*at least 10%*)
6 True (*beef, chicken, potatoes, fruit and vegetables*)

Flow chart completion

5

Answers

7 calcium ascorbate
8 refrigerated trucks/green bags
9 fourteen days

Short answer questions

Refer students to Unit 4, pages 58–59 for revision on approaches to answering short answer questions.

Answers

10 apples, grapes
11 2.2
12 one-quarter, 25%
13 Cameo, Pink Lady

Language focus p107

that-clauses

Aim
When students cite sources in their academic essays, they will need to make wide use of reported speech. In this section, students practise using the structures and vocabulary of reporting and referencing.

Explain that *that* can have the function of joining two parts of a sentence and introducing a clause that reports opinion, facts or attitudes.

This use of *that* should not be confused with the function of *that* in relative clauses (to replace *who, whom* or *which* in defining relative clauses).

Refer students to Unit 7 Grammar, page 175 for a detailed explanation and examples of *that* as a conjunction in reported speech. Explain that some reporting verbs must have a direct object (a person / group / organization), others cannot take a direct object and must be followed by *that*. Students look up reporting verbs in the dictionary and complete the table.

1 Students work in pairs to answer 1–3.

Answers

1 B
2 A
3 C

2 Ask students to underline the verbs in 1–11 before answering the questions individually and comparing their answers with a partner.

Answers

1 It has been proven that *fact*
2 Tests indicate that *opinion*
3 Scientists can confirm that *fact*
4 It is certain that *fact*
5 Results show that *fact*
6 It is interesting that *opinion*
7 In spite of/Despite the fact that *fact* (not a main clause)
8 It is doubtful that *opinion*
9 Many would argue that *opinion*
10 Some believe that *opinion*

3 Ask students to look at Sentence 1 and underline the main verb and the subject.

Explain that sentences in academic writing typically include long noun phrases as subjects. A noun phrase may include a defining clause and several adjectives as well as the subject of the verb. Point out that the structure of a sentence with a long noun phrase as a subject is similar to that of a sentence with a simple noun subject.

In Sentence 2, ask students to underline or circle a defining clause and a place in the subject-noun phrase.

Further practice

Refer students to Photocopiable 7, Exercises 1 and 2 (TB page 115).

4

Answers

1 Authorities on management styles argue that managers exhibit one of two management styles, which are described as 'authoritarian' and 'democratic'.
2 Managers exhibiting an authoritarian style of management believe that people are basically lazy and will avoid work and responsibility.
3 Managers employing a democratic style of management believe that work is natural to people and can be enjoyed.
4 Democratic managers argue that employees will assume as much responsibility as their abilities and their employers will allow.
5 Effective managers recognize that their ability to lead is a direct extension of their personal credibility.

5

Suggested answers

1 W: Peter Chan, the new sales representative, is the man that I was telling you about.
2 R
3 W: The diagram shows unemployment throughout the 1980s in Southern European countries (+ verb).
4 W: In my opinion, the removal of trade barriers would enable developing countries to build strong economies and reduce their dependence on aid.
5 W: It is my opinion that we are on the verge of a breakthrough in information technology which will have a profound impact on the global economy.
6 W: As can be seen, the charts show clearly the number of boys and girls in all levels of education in developing and developed countries (+ verb).
7 W: As we can see, there is only a slight difference between the two countries.
8 W: If we look at all three charts we can see that all levels of education were able to achieve the final target.
9 R

Further practice

Refer students to Unit 7 Vocabulary, page 182.

Vocabulary p109

Aim
As students will write a number of essays during their academic studies, they will need to find alternatives to frequently occurring vocabulary. The *thesaurus* is the most effective way of finding synonyms and parallel expressions. Students need to be aware, however, of the importance of using vocabulary in the correct context.

Synonyms for people

Elicit names of groups of people by profession, for example *medicine, education, sport*. Then ask students to work in pairs with a thesaurus to find alternative descriptions of professions in these groups (doctors = *medical professionals*, teachers = *educators*, coaches = *trainers*).

1 Students complete the table individually and compare their answers with a partner.

Answers

People (in general)	People and work	People and power	People (specific groups)
everyone	the unemployed	politicians	the old/young
the general public	employees	national/ religious	students
leaders	managers	consumers	the middle-aged
individuals	manufacturers	voters	parents
human beings	representatives	celebrities	
entrepreneurs		home owners	
workers		teenagers	
employers			

2

Answers

1 voters
2 entrepreneurs
3 consumers
4 individuals
5 the unemployed
6 everyone (or similar)
7 manufacturers
8 politicians/national leaders
9 workers
10 celebrities

Further practice

Refer students to Photocopiable 7, Exercises 3 and 4 (TB page 115) for further practice of synonyms in context.

3 To increase their understanding of unknown words, students ask a partner to explain the words before checking the meanings in a dictionary.

Speaking p110

1 and 2 You may want to treat each of the topics individually, to give students an opportunity to focus on specific vocabulary.

Topic 1: Jobs

Ask students about any job experience they may have. Note relevant vocabulary on the board. Vocabulary may include: *temporary, part-time, work placement, internship, work experience, weekend/holiday/evening job.*

Students answer questions 1–3, add a question and interview their partner.

Topic 2: Time

Discuss national and personal attitudes to punctuality and time management including the use of electronic diaries and online calendars.

Students answer questions 1–3, add a question and interview their partner.

Predicting the future

Elicit brand names and products. Ask students if they think that brand name products are better than imitations / non-brand products. Ask about experiences with brand names.

3 2.1 Before listening to the model answer, ask students to read the question, make notes of their opinions and discuss their ideas in groups.

Ask students to make a note of possible ways of filling the gaps.

Play the recording for students to complete the text. Answers are underlined in the recording script.

Answers

1 it is highly likely
2 cannot definitely say
3 quite possible
4 most probably

2.1

Well, I think it is highly likely that young people, particularly in my country, will still be buying brand names like Nike and Adidas. Of course I cannot definitely say whether or not this will be the case in other countries. Having said that, it's quite possible that brand names will still be popular amongst young people in Western countries because, if the present is anything to go by, then they will most probably still be trying to follow the latest fashions in the future.

4 and 5 Students work in pairs to complete the table. Discuss answers as a whole class.

Answers

	Certain	Fairly certain	Uncertain
Ex. 4	–	it is highly likely quite possible most probably	cannot definitely say
Ex. 5	4 There is no question in my mind that 7 I can say without a doubt/most definitely that 9 I'm quite/ totally/utterly convinced that	1 There is a strong possibility that 3 It might/ could be the case that 6 There is every chance that	2 I'm not really sure if 5 I think it's debatable whether 8 No one can predict whether 10 It's impossible to say whether/if

6 Monitor students while they discuss the questions in pairs, make notes of their opinions and the degree of certainty of their predictions. Students then form groups of four to exchange ideas.

Reading 2 p111

1 After discussing 1 and 2 in pairs, extend the discussion to the whole class. Make a note of key vocabulary on the board for students to add to their vocabulary bank.

Note completion

2 Ask students to underline the keywords in the notes and scan the text.

Keywords: orders, no scope, expected to, pressure, succeed, too much work.

Answers

1 delegate (the order/s)
2 discretion
3 (corporate) vision
4 judgement
5 delegate more
6 admit defeat

Yes, No, Not Given

3

Answers

7 No (A *Authority is, on the whole…*; B *They are more inclined … to want to query …*)
8 Yes
9 Not Given (The passage does not say that they worry about this.)
10 Yes (paragraphs G and H)

Matching details to paragraphs

4

Aim
These questions require students to find details in the passage. This is often easier for students to do when they have already read the text to find answers to other questions and may remember where the details have been mentioned. For this reason, it's a good idea to advise students to answer these questions (11–15) last, when they have already read the passage to answer other questions.

Students scan for the keywords or synonyms before answering the questions.

Answers

11 H
12 F
13 E
14 G
15 D

Listening 1 p114

Section 2: Prediction

Students work in pairs to answer 1–4 in the Exam Strategy section. Refer students to Unit 2, pages 24–25 to check their answers.

Answers

1 Keep up with the recording. Answer the questions effectively.
2 To try to predict what the recording will be about.
3 Keywords in the question and in the instructions.
4 Words written in bold or capital letters.

1

Aim
It is useful for students to be aware of the rights of people with disabilities in the UK and to be able make comparisons with their own country. In the UK, the legislation to protect the rights of people with disabilities is called the Disability Discrimination Act 2005 (DDA). Children with disabilities are supported by the Special Education Needs and Disability Act 2001 (SENDA).

Check students understand relevant vocabulary by asking for definitions of: *wheelchair access, disability, special needs, discrimination.*

Students discuss their answers to 1–3 and make notes to report back to a discussion with the whole class.

2 2.2 Give students time to read the questions carefully and underline the keywords before listening. Answers are underlined in the recording script.

Short answer questions

Answers

1 holiday jobs
2 informed choices

Sentence completion

Answers

3 plan ahead
4 public areas/public spaces/toilets
5 ramps
6 flexible
7 disabled parking (spaces)/wheelchair accessible entrance/ramp

2.2

Hello and thanks everyone for coming here today. I know it's always a bit stressful going for a job interview, but it's best to be prepared. For any of you who may not know me, my name is Fiona Ogilvy and my job is to offer guidance and support for students with special needs. Now you wouldn't be here today if you weren't interested in finding a job in the holidays so let's get down to it and see what things you need to be looking out for. Most of you, I hope, will be applying for jobs with the companies that have been recommended by the university. The reason for this is that we here at the university, already know these companies and have established good working relationships with them. I've also been to visit all of them and checked out the facilities they have to offer. You really need to make informed choices when you're looking for a job and make sure you know before you even get to the interview stage, that your needs will be met. But I know that some of you are applying for jobs independently and have looked at companies outside the university recommended list so for you it's best to plan ahead and be aware of what it is you may need while you're working. Things that you need to check when you go for an interview are: are there enough toilet facilities and are these easily accessible? Also, you want to check that all the public areas inside the building are barrier-free so you can get direct access to these public spaces whenever you need to. And ask about ramps into the building so you know how many there are and where they are located. These kinds of things are so much more difficult to sort out when you've started work as they take time. But ramps are an absolute must so please make sure you know where they are. Another thing you must make sure of is that the lifts have the correct lowered control panels. Ask if all the lifts have this facility or if it's only certain ones. Now something I think that is often overlooked is working hours. What you want to make sure of is that you get flexitime. This basically means that your working hours are flexible and you can clock on and clock off in times that suit you – within reason of course! Most companies do recognize that it takes much longer for someone in a wheelchair to get on and off buses and trains – public transport can take that much longer so you need to be organized and prepared. And for those of you lucky enough to own a car, check how many disability parking spaces are available. Remember that it's your right to have a disabled parking space. These also need to be near enough to a wheelchair accessible entrance or ramp. OK, are there any questions before we move on?

Table completion

2.3

Answers

8 receptionist
9 10.00 a.m.
10 Tuesday p.m./afternoon
11 local company
12 tea, coffee
13 none/bring packed lunch
14 main hall
15 10.30

2.3

Right, let's move on then. Now I want to talk you through the series of visits to companies which we've got planned for next week. On Monday morning we will be visiting the Lowland Hotel. They have various summer jobs available working as a receptionist or conference organizer in their busy conference centre organizing and setting up conferences. You need to be prepared for working in an office environment and spending quite a bit of time talking on the telephone. The bus leaves for the hotel at 9.00 a.m. so make sure you leave yourself plenty of time to get there. When you arrive at the hotel, please gather in the reception area and wait for someone to take you to your first session, which will be a talk. The talk at the hotel will begin at 10.00 a.m. and then there will be a short tour of the hotel. There will be a light lunch provided which is usually salads and sandwiches. The next place we'll be visiting will be on Tuesday afternoon. We'll be going to visit a little local company that makes handmade paper and cards. For those of you studying art, this may be just what you're looking for. We'll be taken on a tour of the company which lasts 3 hours. The tour will start at 3.30 p.m. and after that you'll have a chance to meet some of the staff. Tea and coffee will also be provided. We have no trips planned for Wednesday, but on Thursday morning we'll be going to Tobago Travel Agency. This is a very popular choice amongst our students because you can get student discounts on holidays. We've booked a coach for this and it'll leave from outside the refectory at

8.00 a.m. You will need to bring a packed lunch for this so please don't forget. There is a little canteen where you can buy hot and cold food, but this is closed on Thursdays. Friday we'll be having representatives from all the companies visiting us so you will have a chance to ask any questions and of course, put your name down on the list if you're interested in working for them over the summer. This event will take place in the main hall next to the library and it'll run from 10.30 until 4.00.

I really hope you make the most of this excellent opportunity to not only earn yourself some extra money, but also to gain experience of what it's like to work. And if you'd like to find out more, then please ask some of the students who worked last year. They're all wearing green badges and will be happy to speak to you afterwards.

Pronunciation p115

Connected speech

1 Elicit responses from students for 1–3 and illustrate linking on the board.

Answers

1 you will agree
2 one of the factors
3 to help answer

2 **Note**: After round lip vowels, for example /u:/ the intrusive sound is /w/.

After spread lip vowels, for example /i:/ the intrusive sound is /j/.

Elicit examples of linking with additional sounds /w/ and /j/ from 1–2.

Answers

1 you w all have
2 we j all have

Students discuss further examples of /w/ and /j/ sounds. Possible examples are:

do w another exercise

go w away

go w and see

see j all your friends

be j out

3 and 4 2.4 Students connect the words in 1–6, then listen and check their answers.

Answers

1 Most of you /w/ I hop[e] will be /j/ applying for jobs with companies the university has recommended.
2 Make sure you know before you /w/ even get to the interview stage, that /j/ your needs will be met.
3 I know that some of you /w/ are applying for jobs independently, so for you it's best to plan ahead and be aware of what it is you may need.
4 Ask if all the lifts have this facility or if it's only certain ones.
5 When /j/ you arrive at the hotel, wait for someone to take /j/ you to /j/ your first session, which will be a talk.
6 The next place we'll be visiting will be /j/ on Tuesday afternoon.

Writing p116

Task 1: Multiple diagrams 1

Explain the question strategy as follows:

Approach 1 = a comparison between two diagrams that measure the same elements

Approach 2 = two separate descriptions of diagrams with a concluding sentence comparing any common elements

The fixed parts define the parameters of the diagram (for example for the table in Exercise 1A these are *country* and *wage*).

Students revise parameters and what is being measured by referring to the diagrams in Unit 1, Exercise 3, page 18 (qualification level and year/the highest qualification for school leavers as a percentage) and Unit 3, Exercises 3–10, pages 51–54, making a note of the parameters in each case.

1 Students decide which approach to use for A and B.

Answers

A: approach 2 = separate description of each + single comparison as the summarizing sentence
B: approach 1 = comparison

2 Students work in pairs to answer 1–5. Refer students to the bar charts in Unit 3, page 54.

Answers

1 This is a horizontal bar chart so the vertical axis has become the horizontal axis.
2 Countries, and % export and % manufacturing.
3 years
4 Both – there are changes over time for different factors.
5 Both approaches are possible, but the former would be better as the charts both measure the same countries across the same times.

3 In pairs, students discuss the answers to 1–5, referring to the bar charts in Exercise 2, page 116.

Answers

Share of global manufacturing
1 US
2 Germany
3 US, China
4 China increasing, US decreasing
5 Overall it can be seen that China's share of global manufacturing is increasing whereas the US's share is decreasing.

Share of world exports
1 US
2 Japan
3 China, Japan
4 China increasing, Japan decreasing
5 Overall it can be seen that China's share of world exports is increasing whereas Japan's share is decreasing.

4 Students write a short (150-word) essay describing the bar charts on page 116. They exchange essays with a partner and compare their partner's answer with Unit 7 Model answer, page 193, underlining key information in both.

Ways of describing data

5 Students write the sentences and discuss their answers in pairs.

6 Students select information from the pie charts and discuss their reasons for choosing particular features for comparison and summary. In pairs, using vocabulary from the Useful language box on page 117, students summarize key features orally.

7

Answers

1 all, most, the (vast) majority, many, equal numbers of, a minority of, (very) few, none
2 Accept any suitable answer.

8

Answers

By industry or by time of work. Time of work would make comparison easier and would be a more logical plan.

Multiple diagrams 2

10 Refer students to the Question Strategy at the beginning of the section to decide which approach to use (approach 2 because the diagrams have different parameters and can only be linked for comparison by gender).

Refer students to the Unit 7 Model answers and comments, page 193.

Study skills p119

Editing your writing

Aim
Students will need to revise, criticize and edit their own writing throughout their academic career. A strategy to enable students to develop a critical approach to their own work is to first develop peer criticism, editing and discussion skills. These can then be applied to students' own writing.

1

Answers

Example 1 is a good writer. Although there are some mistakes (*In contrary*), they do not affect the overall meaning. There is evidence of wide vocabulary use, good grammar and punctuation.

Example 2 is an average writer. There are grammar, punctuation and spelling mistakes. Vocabulary has also been repeated suggesting a more limited vocabulary use. The style in places is inappropriate (*beautiful life*).

Dictionary focus p120

1

Answers

focus on fresh fruits = *focus* + preposition + adjective + noun

a *comparable* influence on the market = article + *comparable* + noun + preposition

McDonald's *exerts* over the produce = noun + *exerts* + preposition + article + noun

approximately the same as/a quarter/10.000 = *approximately* + a figure/a comparison

variation in work patterns = *variation* + preposition+ noun

marked resurgent/differences = *marked* + noun

in developing countries *world-wide* = preposition + adjective + noun + *world-wide*

2

Answers

Accept any suitable answer.

1 marked 2 world-wide 3 focus

3 Students check the meanings of the words in the dictionary and add them to their vocabulary bank.

Further practice

Refer students to Photocopiable 7, Exercise 5 (TB page 116).

8 Art and the city

Content overview

Themes

The main themes of Unit 8 are architecture, town planning, visual art, funding for artists and cultural facilities for the public.

Listening
- a talk about research
- a dialogue about research into town planning
- a lecture on contemporary art

Reading
- a newspaper article about organic architecture

Writing
- argument and opinions about art and architecture

Exam related activities

Listening

Section 3	Multiple-choice questions
	Short answer questions
	Note completion
Section 4	Multiple-choice questions
	Sentence completion
	Short answer questions

Reading

Matching: people and descriptions
Summary completion (no list)
Sentence completion (from a list)

Writing

Task 2 Balanced argument and opinion essays

Speaking

Part 2 Structuring a short talk

Language development

Language focus

Linking words
Cause and effect
Concession

Vocabulary

Buildings
Prepositions
Visual arts / performing arts

Skills development

Reading

Distinguishing fact from opinion

Writing

Refuting opposing arguments
Conclusions

Listening

Listening for signposting

Study skills

Spelling

Dictionary focus

The arts

Warm up p120

Ask students to identify the buildings in the photos and locate them on a map of the world. Have any students seen these buildings?

Answers

Sagrada Familia – Barcelona, Spain
Acropolis – Athens, Greece
Empire State Building – New York, USA
Casa Mila – Barcelona, Spain
Sydney Opera House – Sydney, Australia
Dubai Sail Building – Dubai

1–3 Elicit answers to Exercise 1. Revise *used to be*. Responses to Exercises 2 and 3 could lead to a revision of comparatives and superlatives (Unit 3).

Reading p120

Distinguishing fact and opinion

Aim
A critical approach to reading is an important part of academic study. Students need to identify writers' viewpoints so as to be able to discuss their premises and arguments, and recognize the facts on which these arguments are based.

1 Students work in pairs to answer 1 and 2. They refer to the dictionary for unfamiliar words. Students write sentences to illustrate alternative uses of the adjectives in the box.

2 Elicit possible definitions of *organic* (*connected with living things*).

Answers

organic architecture = *individualistic, eccentric, magnificent*

The use of *magnificent* suggests his opinion is mainly positive.

3 Point out that adjectives such as *strange* and *extraordinary* and verbs such as *seem* and *look* signal that the writer is expressing an opinion. Remind students of the expressions signalling opinion which were practised in Unit 7 Language focus, pages 107–109.

Answers

1 fact
2 opinion
3 fact
4 opinion
5 opinion

4 Ask students to scan the passage and underline the information in the sentences in Exercise 3 before checking with a partner.

Answers

The information in all of the sentences but 2 is mentioned.

5 Refer students to Photocopiable 2, Exercises 2 and 3 (TB pages 107–108) to revise the criteria for deciding the purpose of a text.

Answers

1 C
2 B

Matching: people and descriptions

6 Students work in pairs to discuss and answer these questions.

Answers

1 A, E
2 C, D
3 A
4 C

Summary completion (No list)

7 Ask students to check their answers with a partner after completing the summary individually.

Answers

5 natural
6 stone
7 (two) courtyards
8 a Dali painting
9 roof/roofline
10 interiors
11 the/his design

Sentence completion (From a list)

8

Answers

12 C
13 E
14 A
15 B

Language focus p124

Linking expressions

Ask students to match the linking words in Exercise 1 (*in addition, in order to, however, so, because, for example)* with functions a–f in Unit 8 Grammar, Use (2), page 176.

Answers

1 d
2 e
3 c
4 a
5 f
6 b

1

Answers

1 f
2 b
3 c
4 e
5 a
6 d

2 This exercise can be used to cross-check answers to Exercise 1.

Answers

1 because
2 so
3 in order to
4 however
5 for example
6 in addition

3

Answers

1 Reason: *because of*
2 Result: *thus, therefore*
3 Purpose: *so that, so as (not) to*
4 Contrast: *although, nevertheless, in spite of, despite, whereas*
5 Example: *for instance*
6 Addition: *as well as, furthermore*

4 Refer students to Form Unit 8 Grammar, page 176 and elicit examples to check understanding of uses of *because, despite* and *since* as conjunctions. Elicit uses of *however* and *for example,* as adverbials that link sentences.

Answers

1 although, as well as, because, because of, despite, for example, for instance, in order to, so that, in order to, since, so, so as (not) to, whereas
2 for example, furthermore, however, in addition, thus, therefore, nevertheless

5 Students work in pairs to discuss 1–3. Go through answers with the whole class.

Answers

(some expressions can be followed by more than one form)
1 Clause: *although, because, for example, for instance, furthermore, however, in addition, in order that/so that, since, so, thus, therefore, nevertheless, whereas*
2 Noun: *as well as, because of, despite, for example*
3 Verb: *so that, in order to/so as to*

6 Students rewrite the sentences in pairs and compare answers with another pair.

Answers

1 Although architects should express themselves freely, their work must also be practical.
2 Despite the stress of living in a city, there are still many advantages to doing so.
3 Because of concerns about the environment, organic architecture will probably remain popular.
4 The city invested in a new sports complex so as to encourage more people to exercise and get fit.

7 Students create a paragraph by completing the sentences. They then practise giving a short talk to their partner.

Further practice

Refer students to the sentence completion exercise in Unit 8 Grammar, page 176.

Vocabulary 1 p125

Elicit vocabulary for accommodation by asking students where they live in their home country and / or (if applicable) in the UK. Discuss the most popular forms of housing in students' home country(ies) and the reasons for this. Discuss the differences between rural and urban housing and between traditional and modern housing. All new vocabulary should be written on the board for students to add to their vocabulary bank.

1

Answers

1 villa
2 studio flat
3 apartment block
4 bungalow
5 basement flat
6 high rise

2 Students label the illustration and discuss their answers in pairs.

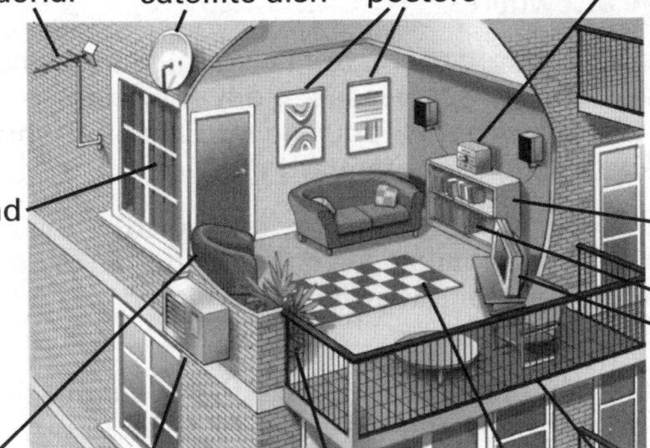

3 Students make notes for one minute before speaking to each other about a room in their house.

Further practice

For further practice of collocations, refer students to Unit 8 Vocabulary, page 183.

Listening p126

Section 3: Analysing multiple-choice options

1 Elicit possible answers to the question and discuss reasons for students' choices.

2 2.5 Play the recording and ask students to choose the answer (from Exercise 1) given by the student being interviewed. Elicit possible reasons for choices.

Answers

B

2.5

Well, I think research is important for us as individual researchers. We need to know that our ideas and suggestions are valid. But more importantly, it's for others. We cannot prove our ideas effectively unless we look back at the past, to research that has been done before. We then check past evidence with present day evidence to see if it correlates. So without research being done, ideas will not be made valid.

3 Students read the recording script and discuss the reasons why A and C (in Exercise 1) are incorrect.

Answers

A is incorrect because *past evidence* must be checked against *present day evidence*.

C is incorrect because it says that *more importantly* research is *for others*.

4 2.6 Brainstorm vocabulary associated with research. Make sure it includes: *project, valid, research question, investigate, evidence, focus, thesis*.

Answers

B, E, F (in any order)

2.6

[M = Miwako; E = Enrique]

M: So Enrique, have you started your research project on cities yet?

E: I've done a bit of reading around the topic and made a few notes, but if I'm honest about it, I really haven't done as much as I'd have liked to because I'm finding it a bit difficult.

M: You don't know how relieved I am to hear you say that! I feel the same way. I think the key is to be able to make valid research questions.

E: You're probably right about that. Didn't we have some lectures on how to write research questions? I think it was towards the beginning of the term.

M: Yes, we did. I've got my notes somewhere in this file. I tell you what, why don't we look at the notes together and then try and come up with some research questions. At least that would be a good starting point, give us some sense of where we're going with this.

E: Brilliant idea! Let's get started. OK, from what I remember, <u>a good research question is all about knowing from the outset what it is you're trying to find out.</u>

M: Yes, and now that I'm looking at my notes again, I see I've written here that it's to do with understanding and evaluation. So understanding a particular issue and evaluating any problems around it. And of course, a very important part is not overlooking any research that has already been done. Past research is just as important as what is being done now.

E: It's a bit, I suppose, like looking at the research that's already been done and seeing if it agrees or disagrees with your own ideas.

M: Mmm ... sure, I hear what you're saying, but to do that properly you have to have a clear idea in your head what your own research question is and by that I mean specific areas you want to focus on. Let's face it, there's so much information out there and we can't possibly include it all in 2,000 words.

E: Don't remind me! The thought of writing 2,000 words at the moment seems like a huge mountain to climb.

M: I know, but let's try to make a start. I think we're meant to be identifying what makes a successful city and also try explain why there has been such a steady population movement of people from rural to urban areas. But I'm a bit confused because I don't think this is meant to be the main focus of our research.

E: Mmm ... perhaps that's why the lecturer said we need to write questions and that must be our starting point.

M: OK ... well, what we're investigating is more than simply what elements make a city successful, but we're also trying to offer possible explanations so we have two questions: why do people want to move to cities and why do people choose to live in them.

Short answer questions

Answers

4 2,000 words
5 write questions

Note completion

2.7

Answers

6 good job opportunities/good job prospects
7 standard of living
8 green spaces
9 good night life
10 sense of community

2.7

[M = Miwako; E = Enrique]

E: OK then, I think the first issue concerning successful cities must be the economy. People move to cities for better job prospects and successful cities are cities that have thriving economies.

M: That's true enough, it does mean that cities can offer good job opportunities, which seems to me to suggest that a city will only be successful if it attracts the right kind of people to work there.

E: What kind of person are you talking about?

M: Well, I suppose I'm referring to the skilled labour force. You know, the idea that up and coming young people will move to cities, settle there, maybe buy property and so that city will get the most talented, creative minds. But if a city doesn't offer this, then obviously it will lose out as university leavers will choose elsewhere.

E: You could be right there, but I also think that when cities encourage businesses to develop then you obviously have money pouring into the city, which can raise the general standard of living.

M: So we've definitely got a question worth investigating, but apart from the economic factor, I think another point worth mentioning is the environment.

E: Sure, we can research areas like the quality of the air, how clean it is and then there's traffic ... um ... is there too much traffic, how is it controlled and also the issues of noise pollution and how the city manages its waste. Um ... oh, and I nearly forgot, the environment includes green spaces, like parks.

M: Those are all valid points, but I think you've overlooked the whole issue of beauty.

E: Beauty? Are you sure? What's beauty got to do with the environment?

M: Well, don't you think if you were deciding whether or not you would live in a city, your first impressions would be made with your eyes? So the buildings in a city are really important. If the entire city looks like a concrete jungle, then it's unlikely to make people want to live there, is it? I think successful cities are those which have managed to strike a balance between old buildings and new ones. So of course, you'd have some buildings reflecting more modern architecture, but others that haven't lost their character and still represent the past.

E: You're right, actually. I've often thought that buildings tell a story ... I mean you can tell the history of a place by looking at the buildings.

M: I know exactly what you mean and let's not forget that the environment includes cultural aspects so for example, what's the cultural life like? For me, a successful city will be attractive because it will have lots to offer, like a good night life and a wide variety of places to visit in the day like museums and galleries, places like that.

E: True, true. My own view is that some cities have an energy about them ... they're exciting to be in.

M: And other cities are the opposite! Well, we've covered so much ground here, but I think there's one final aspect we should research.

E: What's that then?

M: The social aspect because let's face it, cities are made up of people.

E: They are and surely a successful city would be one where there is a sense of community, a place where people would feel safe and want to raise families in.

M: This topic is limitless ...

Section 4

1 and 2 2.8

Suggested answers

1 the topic of the lecture (contemporary art)
2 point of view/focus
3 Firstly ... (art as something made and appreciated)
Secondly ... (art's relationship with society)
4 a definition (contemporary art reflects a particular time in history)

Remind students that they should follow the signposts while they listen to the recording. If they pause for too long on one question, they may miss the answer to the next one.

2.8

Welcome to this series of lectures on interpreting contemporary art. This morning I'd like to look at the whole issue of contemporary art, what it is, how do we interpret it, what are its uses and does art, in effect, have any advantages or disadvantages for society. I think at this point, it's important for me to clarify that I am looking at art from two main perspectives. Firstly, art as something made by and appreciated by individuals and secondly, art's relationship with society as it is society that supports, protects and encourages art. And I'm hoping that this lecture will act as a springboard for you to revisit your own artistic experiences and question your own ideas of what contemporary art means. Throughout this series of lectures, I'll be looking at various examples of art to illustrate my points.

However, if at any point I show you an example which is unfamiliar, then please tell me as it is imperative that you be able to use your past experiences so that you can check to see if your ideas agree with mine. So if you have not seen a particular work of art before, then this will not work and let me remind you now, that at the end of these lectures, you will be given a written assignment which will consist of a 2,500-word critical essay.

OK, so what is contemporary art? Well, my view is that contemporary art reflects a particular time in history. In terms of Western civilization, this is the period that became known as the Renaissance, which began roughly in 1450.

3 2.9

Multiple choice

Answers

1 B
2 B
3 A

Sentence completion

Answers

4 1789
5 1920
6 academic
7 businessmen/famous people
8 graffiti

Short answer questions

Answers

9 public buildings
10 violence/violence in society
11 feelings, attitudes

2.9

But this becomes confusing as the modern era is also considered to be from 1789, from the time of the French Revolution. Added to this are modern ideas and modern art that developed from 1890. This period has also been called the 'turn of the century.' To try and somehow bring all these periods together, I shall define contemporary art as any art created from 1920 up until the present day.

Turning now to the question of whether or not art is useful for society ... er ... well, when we look back at the history of the West, we can see that there has been a tradition, especially in Western Europe, of art that was official. This meant that the government sponsored or subsidized the art. It could be said therefore that art has a cultural use in that it can represent both the culture and history of a country ... and ... um ... let's remember what I said earlier, that this is both the history and culture of a particular time. Now the disadvantage of this kind of official art is that it tends to be academic and, by that I mean it is art that requires the person looking at it to be educated in art, at least to some extent. So it seems to me that this restricts this type of art to a particular social group and whether you agree with this concept or not will depend on if you believe that art should be accessible to everyone.

Of course, with the rapid developments in technology and advertising, the television, computer and various forms of digital media, art has changed and although there will always be a need for art to be subsidized by governments, we see today art forms that are surviving on individual subsidy. Sometimes this is through the support of wealthy patrons such as businessmen or famous people. But it also operates on a more simple level. Er ... I refer here to the art that is done on walls and in streets, sometimes called amateur art, but it is the art of graffiti and it is now accepted as an art form in itself. So here we come to what I see as another advantage for society in that art is a means by which people can express their ideas, their feelings. Of course, in the case of graffiti, there is much debate as to whether the advantages outweigh the more negative side which is when graffiti artists paint on public buildings. This creates unnecessary expense and also damages these buildings which are meant for public use. We will be looking at some examples of this later on. Now many critics of contemporary art have pointed to art that is often violent and ... er ... even obscene. But I would like to suggest that such art is not meant to only shock us. It also has the element of exposure so it can teach us about the violence in society. This then brings us to another advantage of art: it can raise awareness, help us see things in a different light. The disadvantage of this is that art can be dangerous ... um ... what I'm saying here is that if we accept that contemporary art has the power to influence our feelings and attitudes, then we have to accept that art can evoke negative feelings like anger as much as it can give us feelings of hope and peace.

But art is, after all, about us so it can be about our beliefs and our behaviour and, as human beings, we possess both positive and negative traits. I'd like to show you some slides now to illustrate what I've been talking about ...

Further practice

Refer students to Photocopiable 8, Exercises 1 and 2 (TB page 117) for practice in using discourse markers.

Vocabulary 2 p129

1 Students work in pairs to classify art forms.

Answers

1 place, performing arts
2 art form, performing arts
3 art form, performing arts
4 place, visual arts
5 art form, visual arts
6 place, visual arts
7 art form, performing arts
8 art form, performing arts
9 art form, visual arts
10 art form, visual arts
11 art form, visual arts
12 place, performing arts

2 and 3 Students discuss art forms they are familiar with, especially those most popular in their country. They make notes for a one-minute talk about their experience with visual or performing arts and then give their talk to a small group.

Answers

Exercise 2: literature, poetry, novels, multimedia, library, blogs

Speaking p129

Structuring what you say

Aim

The ability to recognize and use signposting language will be of considerable use when students attend lectures in their subject speciality and lead seminar discussions.

1 Students match the expressions and discuss their answers with a partner.

Answers

1 B/C
2 C
3 A
4 C
5 B
6 B
7 A
8 B
9 C
10 A

2 Students prepare their talk and then speak to their partner.

Topic A: Buildings

Elicit examples of important national buildings with explanations of why they are important (historically, politically, architecturally).

Students prepare a one minute talk on an important building and interview each other.

Topic B: Works of Art

Elicit examples of important national works of art. Ask students to describe the form, the work of art, and the place where it can be found or seen. Have students seen this work personally?

3 2.10 Before students listen to the model answer, ask them to look again at the expressions in Exercise 1.

As they listen to the recording, students check the signposting expressions from Exercise 1.

Answers

8, 6, 9 (the expressions are underlined in recording script 2.10)

2.10

Um ... the best example I can think of is the *Mona Lisa*. It's really a famous painting, but that's not why I like it. I saw it in the Louvre Museum when I was on holiday last year. Uh ... of course, every tourist likes to go and see famous art, but I must admit that I was surprised the effect the painting had on me. There was something about the way her face was painted. Um ... she seems to be smiling, but in quite a sad way. And I couldn't decide if she was looking at me or not! I remember standing there for a long time just staring at that face. I believe that art is quite important because of the way it changes your perspective on things. For me, this means that it helps me see things in a different way. Um ... ultimately I feel that art not only preserves our history and culture, but can also broaden our horizons and make us see life from a different angle.

Writing p130

Task 2: Review balanced argument and opinion essays

Aim
Students will be expected to write discursive essays as part of their academic studies. They should understand that although they may hold a strong opinion on a topic, their arguments will be strengthened by recognizing and refuting opposing points of view.

1 Students complete the paragraphs and discuss their answers with a partner.

Answers

1 reject
2 supports
3 introduction
4 opposing
5 refute
6 conclusion

A = opinion essay, B = a balanced argument essay

2 Students read the statement about art and poverty and mark their opinion on the scale.

Students then form small groups and discuss their opinions giving reasons and examples to support their ideas.

Answers

1 B 2 A

Refuting opposing arguments

3 Review *in spite of* + clause, *despite* + noun/gerund by eliciting examples from students.

Answers

Giving opinions	Refuting opinions
There is no doubt that	Although ..., it does not necessarily follow that
The evidence for ... is undeniable	In spite of/Despite the fact that
It appears to be the case that	While it is true to say that
	Nevertheless
	The fact that ... does not necessarily mean that
	It may be correct to say that ... but
	Having said that
	Despite having

4 Students write their answers individually and discuss them with a partner.

Suggested answers

1 Although ... it does not necessarily mean that ... / The fact that ... does not necessarily mean that ...
2 Despite the fact that ... / It may be correct to say that ... but ...
3 Having said that ...
4 Despite the fact that ... / It may be correct to say that ... but ...
5 Although ... it does not necessarily mean that ... / The fact that ... does not necessarily mean that ...

5 The range of responses will require correction by the teacher. Incorrect sentences can be collated and used in a future class for peer and group correction.

6

Answers

Balanced argument essay

Use the following table to point out that a balanced essay can be structured in two main ways. Get students to check each other's answers for structure.

	Structure 1	Structure 2
	Introduction	Introduction
Para. 1	Argument For: point 1 + support	Argument For: point 1 + support Argument Against: point 1 + support
Para. 2	Argument For: point 2 + support	Argument For: point 2 + support Argument Against: point 2 + support
Para. 3	Argument Against: point 1 + support	Argument For: point 3 + support Argument Against: point 3 + support
Para. 4	Argument Against: point 2 + support	Argument For: point 4 + support Argument Against: point 4 + support

7 Students make notes of the main points of the model answer and compare them with another student's.

Answers

Para. 1: public art attracts good workers and tourists

Para. 2: poor infrastructure leads to economic decline

Students discuss their answers to 1–3.

Answers

2 the body of the essay

3 *Although putting a focus on ..., it does not necessarily mean that ...*

For instance, the popularity of London ... despite the city having ...

Accept any suitable alternatives. For example:

Despite the fact that putting a focus on infrastructure seems sensible, it does not ...

In addition, the fact that a city ... does not necessarily mean that it will be ...

Further practice

For further practice of planning and writing argument/ refutation essays, refer students to Photocopiable 8, Exercises 3 and 4 (TB page 118).

Writing conclusions

Aim

Discursive writing should lead to a conclusion which should comprise a summary of the main points proposed during the essay, an evaluation of the argument and a final comment which brings the argument to a close. The concluding paragraph should not include any new information. It can, however, suggest potential areas of research and future developments.

8 Students work in pairs to compare conclusions A, B and C using the self-check questions in the box.

Answers

Conclusion A: 1 Not really. The first sentence does sum up the issue under discussion but lacks a *To conclude* phrase. 2 Yes. 3 Yes. 4 Yes. 5 No.

Conclusion B: 1 Yes. 2 Yes. 3 Yes. 4 Yes. 5 No. This is the best conclusion.

Conclusion C: 1 No. The writer begins by introducing a new point – this looks like another paragraph from the body of the essay rather than a conclusion. 2 No. 3 Yes. 4 Yes. 5 Yes. A new idea is presented which should have gone into the body of the essay.

Note: Explain that it is not essential to use discourse markers to indicate the conclusion, but they do prepare the reader for final comments. Alternative introductory phrases for a conclusion include: *It can be said, therefore, ... It may be reasonable to say that ..., We can see from these arguments that ...*

9

Answers

Introducing the conclusion: *In the final analysis, To summarize, On balance, Overall*

Stating the final decision/conclusion or recommendation: *Consequently, Thus*

10

Aim

Group discussion is a productive means of generating ideas for essays and encouraging students to expand on their thinking by giving explanations and examples.

Divide students into groups and refer them to the model answers for Unit 2 (page 189) or Unit 4 (pages 190–191). Ask students to cover the conclusions and read the essays. Students give their own conclusions orally to the class before writing them and comparing them with the model conclusions.

Further practice

11 Students discuss the topic in groups and make notes of opinions and ideas. They write an essay outline and discuss it with a partner before writing the essay. Point out that in the IELTS exam students will need to generate ideas, make a plan and write the essay in 40 minutes.

12 Students read the model answers (pages 194–195) and underline or highlight the main arguments and supporting points. In pairs, students exchange essays, compare their partner's essay with the model answers and discuss differences.

Study skills p135

Improving your spelling

1 Elicit spelling strategies from students.

Answers

1 follow a particular spelling rule
2 write words down
3 use an English dictionary
4 write words in a vocabulary book

2

Answers

1 m o d a (accommodation)
2 e u (queue)
3 y c h (psychology)
4 r a b l (considerable)
5 g r a p h (geographical)
6 r a r (library)
7 o n m (environment)
8 e s s (necessary)
9 p o r t u (opportunity)
10 l e n n (millennium)
11 c o r (according)
12 y s i (physical)

Dictionary focus p135

1

Answers

1 painting
2 music
3 sculpture
4 literature
5 theatre
6 dance
7 poetry
8 cinema

2 Students check the meanings of the words in the dictionary and add them to their vocabulary bank.

9 Tomorrow's world

Content overview

Themes

Unit 9 focuses on issues related to population growth and sustainability. Predictions about the future of the planet, the development of technology and the availability of natural resources are also considered.

Listening
- a radio programme about electronic equipment
- a lecture on nanotechnology

Reading
- an article about population growth

Writing
- describing illustrations and maps

Exam related activities

Listening

Section 2	Dates and numbers
	Sentence completion
	Note completion
Section 4	Summary completion
	Diagram completion
	Sentence completion

Reading

Yes, No, Not Given questions
Matching: people with arguments

Writing

Task 1	Describing illustrations
	Maps

Speaking

Part 1	Expressing likes and dislikes

Language development

Language focus

Expressing the future: probability
Hypothetical situations

Vocabulary

Academic vocabulary
Prefixes

Skills development

Reading

Identifying the writer's purpose
Identifying arguments

Writing

Description and definition

Listening

Listening for dates and numbers

Pronunciation

Weak forms

Study skills

Understanding question task words

Dictionary focus

Linking devices

Warm up p136

Brainstorm the topic of each graph: population growth, prosperity and CO_2 emissions, to create mind maps on the board. Vocabulary should include: *developing, industrial countries, life expectancy, birth control, urbanization, overcrowding, wealth, production, industry, rural, agriculture, trade, sustainable, environment, global warming, ozone layer, carbon emissions, pollution, alternative fuels, nuclear, wind, wave, solar power, rain forest.*

Students discuss the graphs in pairs before joining a class discussion predicting future trends in each graph.

Answers

Graph 1: 1 it doubled 2 it could rise slightly and then fall; rise slightly and stabilize/level out; rise sharply 3 rising/falling birth rates, increased life expectancy, improvements in medical care, climate change and natural disaster; disease/epidemics such as AIDS

Graph 2: 4 extreme poverty will have disappeared by 2020; the average income on the planet will have increased by 2060 5 developing countries, for example in Africa

Graph 3: 6a emissions of fossil fuels doubled 6b we began to emit more CO_2 than the planet could absorb 7 burning fossils such as oil and coal 8 contributes to greenhouse effect and climate change 9 use cleaner fuels; sustainable/renewable sources of energy, etc.

Reading p136

Identifying the writer's purpose

Remind students that it is usually possible to identify the purpose of a paragraph from the first sentence. Ask students to underline the words that indicate:

- change (*From the beginning ... to*)
- an opinion (*An enduring myth is ...*)
- a comparison (*... behind that of ...*)
- a prediction (*forecasts*)

Answers

1 D
2 C
3 A
4 B

1 Explain *human carrying capacity* (the number of people which the earth can support).

Answers

The answer is A.

A The writer's opinion is quite clearly expressed in the passage. Although opposing points of view are mentioned, these are refuted.
B The problem of sustainability is discussed but solutions are not presented.
C Causes and effects are mentioned but these are used to support the writer's view.
D Advantages and disadvantages are not mentioned.

Yes, No, Not Given

2 Students work in pairs to find sections of the text which answer questions 2–7.

Answers

2 Not Given (para. 2) He mentions that this is a point of view held by some but doesn't say whether he agrees or disagrees.
3 No (para. 5)
4 Yes (para. 6)
5 Yes (para. 9)
6 No (para. 9)
7 Not Given (para. 7) This is presented as an unanswered question.

Matching: Identification of arguments

3 and 4 Students work in pairs to answer questions 9–15.

Answers

8 D
9 C
10 A
11 E
12 B
13 D
14 B

Vocabulary 1 p139

Academic vocabulary

Aim
In academic writing, it is important for students to use an appropriate register, much of which depends on their choice of vocabulary. The Academic Word List is a useful vocabulary source and can be found on http://www.vuw.ac.nz/lals/research/awl/

1

Answers

1 define
2 assume
3 estimated
4 concept
5 assessment
6 approach
7 establish
8 indicator
9 factor
10 distribution
11 economic
12 significantly

2

Answers

1 assumption
2 conceive
3 definition
4 defining
5 distribute
6 economy/economics
7 economize
8 economically
9 establishment
10 established
11 indicate
12 significance
13 signify
14 significant

Further practice

For practice in summarizing, paraphrasing and using academic vocabulary, refer students to Photocopiable 9, Exercise 1 (TB page 119).

Language focus p140

Expressing the future: probability

Refer students to Unit 9 Grammar, page 177.

1 Students discuss the questions in pairs before forming small groups to confirm their answers.

Answers

1 certainty: *will, definitely, won't*
probability/possibility: *probably, may, might*
2 i–c, ii–e, iii–d, iv–b, v–a

2 Ask students to discuss these questions in pairs, referring to Unit 9 Grammar, page 177.

Answers

1, 2 i–f (future continuous, *will be* + present participle)
ii–g (future perfect, *will* + *have* + past participle)
3 may, might, could

3

Answers

1 will be living
2 will rise/will have risen
3 may reach/might reach/could reach/could have reached
4 probably won't be
5 will probably be

4 Ask students to discuss a–e in small groups, make a note of their predictions and report back to the whole class for further discussion. Remind students that they should always support their opinions / predictions with reasons.

5 Students work in pairs to discuss a–b.

Further practice

Students complete the sentences in Unit 9 Grammar, page 177.

Refer students to Unit 9 Vocabulary, Exercise 1, page 183 to practise different word forms expressing probability.

Listening 1 p141

Section 2: Listening for dates and numbers

1 and 2 2.11 Students practise saying the dates in pairs and check their answers with the recording. Remind students that they can say: *February the ninth* or *the ninth of February*. (In the US, *February nine* is also common.)

2.11

1 February the 9th 2009
2 the 18th of December 2012
3 the 9th of February 2006
4 53 88 2017
5 54 999 420

3 2.12 Students listen and write down the numbers. They then read the recording script on page 204 and discuss the reasons for the correct answers.

2.12

1 1760
2 763 0029
3 30
4 50
5 1860
6 15
7 1550
8 80
9 13
10 2016

4 2.13

Answers

(accept any correct form)
1 12.06
2 4/40/14/12
3 2014/120 billion/19(%)
4 1958/150
5 1960/1960s/16
6 18.11/98,217/1997
7 237 5550/344 4533

2.13

1 Some of the first more advanced mobile phones were introduced into high street shops in December 2006, just before Christmas.
2 It would not be true to say that he rode a bicycle from the age of 4 to 40, because when he was 14 he broke his leg, which meant he didn't ride for at least 12 months.
3 The company forecast that by 2014 there will be at least 120 billion children buying their computer game, an increase of about 19%, which is not as much as they had hoped for.
4 The first satellite was launched in 1958 and there are probably now over 150 still in operation.
5 He graduated from university in the1960s and never dreamt that his invention would still be used 16 years later.
6 On the 18th November, 98,217 people visited the website and voted for the movie *Titanic*, first released in 1997.
7 I'd love you to give me a call sometime. I know you've got my old number, 237 5550, but I've got a new mobile now so my number's changed to 344 4533.

5 2.14 Explain that the radio programme that students will hear is about inventions and their importance. Elicit examples of inventions.

Ask students to discuss the following questions in pairs and write down their own opinions before they listen to the recording.

1 What do *you* think is the greatest invention?

2 Put the following inventions in order of importance from 1–5: *computer, radio, mobile phone, bicycle, Internet.*

Students read through the questions. Play the recording. The correct answers are underlined in the recording script below.

Sentence completion

Answers

1 2,000
2 65%
3 1818
4 the 1890s

Note completion

Answers

5 42%
6 digital photography
7 military network
8 find information/send emails
9 5%
10 1906
11 the Internet
12 type documents

2.14

Good morning. This is Jane Frost with this morning's edition of *Wake up with Frost*. As you all know, for the last week we've been running a survey trying to find out what you, the listeners, think is the greatest invention of the last 200 years. The response has been amazing, double the amount we had last year so thanks to all of you for taking part. We've had about 2,000 responses online and about the same on our phone lines. The lines are now closed and this morning I can announce what the results were. So here it is ... you, the listeners, have chosen as the greatest technological invention of the past 200 years, and let me not forget to mention that 65% of you voted for this, it's the bicycle! Yes, the bicycle, first invented in 1818 and, would you believe it, the first bicycle was made of wood. The second bicycle had iron wheels … I cannot imagine what that must have been like to ride. It would have kept you fit at any rate. But for me, the best thing about the bicycle was what it did for women's rights. Yes, in the 1890s it was the bicycle that meant women could change their clothing, start wearing trousers or pantaloons as they were known. Before then women's clothes had been really uncomfortable and, I'd imagine, quite difficult to breathe in. So thanks to the ordinary bicycle, it was not only the man who wore the trousers in a home. Instead women could now feel far more equal to their male contemporaries. And I'm sure you'll agree, the bicycle is a great way to get regular exercise and of course, it's is much better for the environment. And today over one billion people all over the world ride bicycles and for some, it's their only means of getting around from A to B. So to all you bicycle riders out there … keep up the good work! Coming in a close second, with 42% is the computer. I found out something interesting about the computer which is that really, this word first meant someone who did mathematical calculations. Of course, today with the development of the personal computer, computers are being used for everything from home use, to business and even digital photography. I don't know about you, but I can't imagine life without a computer now. I guess, closely related to the computer is the Internet and this got 12% of your votes. Maybe, like myself, many of you might think of the Internet as being the World-Wide Web, but actually the web is only one part of the Internet. The Internet began as part of the United States military network, but it later began to be used by businesses and academic institutions. Of course today, the Internet has so many uses. We use it for shopping online and entertainment as well as to find information and send emails. But sadly, there is a darker side to the Internet and some of you have sent me emails about this.

Finally, with 5% of your votes, is the radio. We think the radio was invented by Marconi in 1898 and he opened his first radio or 'wireless' factory in the United Kingdom in 1898. In 1906, a man called Reginald Fessenden gave the first radio broadcast from Massachusetts. Ships could hear him at sea and apparently he played the violin. As yet, listeners, I've spared you from having to listen to my guitar playing. But certainly radio is still important. Let's not forget that it was by radio that the *Titanic* sent signals to other ships. And with the popularity of TV today, I was secretly pleased so many of you had still placed importance on the radio. So there you have it … the results of our survey. I think there are still important inventions that were not chosen but deserve a mention: nuclear power and of course, communications satellite, something which I am certain will continue to change the face of how we communicate with each other over both long and short distances. In fact, for me, the mobile phone is one of the greatest inventions of the last 200 years. If I think back to my first phone and then I look at what is happening now. Children born today will probably be more likely to have their first experience of the Internet on a mobile phone screen rather than a computer monitor. Some of the new mobiles that are now being sold make it just as easy and as quick to find information on the web as on a computer. And let's not forget that mobiles now have digital cameras, word processing facilities, so you can type all your documents, and even personal organizers. I think it's quite possible that the mobile may even replace computers one day.

Writing 1 p143

Task 1: Describing illustrations

Aim

Writing detailed descriptions is useful practice for giving precise definitions of terms, a necessary step before discussing concepts in seminars and academic writing.

Elicit a description of a classroom object. Classify vocabulary suggested by students into: name of the object, material, shape, component parts and purpose. Elicit and pre-teach further vocabulary under each category.

Choose an object that has two or more functioning parts and ask students to explain how it works (for example a CD player, tape recorder). Provide vocabulary as needed. This may include: goes + preposition, opens, closes, turns, spins.

1

Answers

a wallet or purse

2

Answers

1 A
2 C
3 A
4 D

3 Students work in pairs to describe and draw objects for each other. To reinforce the vocabulary of description, students can write detailed descriptions of equipment, buildings and well-known public figures for the class to identify.

4 Students look at the illustrations and decide on the main features to be compared before writing their summaries. Remind students of the structure of a Task 1 essay by referring them to Unit 1, page 20.

5 After completing the gaps in the model essay, students underline the descriptions of the main features of the mobile phones in the model essay and compare them with the main features in their own essay.

Suggested answers

1 is used to
2 consists of
3 height/length
4 weight
5 versatility
6 capability/function
7 useful/necessary for
8 versatile/capable

Further practice

6 In pairs, students discuss the main features of the diagram and the possible points of comparison before answering the question in writing.

7 Students refer to the model answer on page 195.

Speaking p146

Expressing likes and dislikes

1 Students write three questions each for questions 1–4 before interviewing each other in pairs and discussing the topics in groups

2 and 3 2.15 and 2.16 Students discuss the topic of shops in pairs, and make a note of their own likes and dislikes. They then listen to the recording and complete the table with expressions that show preference. They can check their answers in the recording script on page 205.

Explain that these answers are longer than some IELTS answers, which are usually 30 seconds long. However, the aim is to see how the vocabulary can be used in context and candidates in the Speaking module are never penalized for giving answers that are too long.

Answers

Like: *I really love, I simply adore ..., One of my favourite things is ..., I feel really passionately about this ..., totally amazing*

Dislike: *I just can't stand ..., I really hate ..., There's nothing worse than ...(+ verb + -ing), I'm totally disgusted by ...*

2.15

Candidate 1: I really love my little local corner shop. I simply adore being able to shop there, just because it's so convenient. I mean ... it's got all the basics, bread, milk, washing-up liquid and other things like that. One of my favourite things is being able to pop down on a Sunday and buy the papers and some fresh bread. I know some of my friends think it's too expensive, but I think it's worth every penny. And I think little shops are such an important part of local life and so we should support them.

I feel really passionately about this because I've seen many small businesses being forced to close because they can't compete with larger chain stores. Anyway, my local store is totally amazing. I certainly couldn't live without it!

2.16

Candidate 2: Mmm ... well, I usually try and shop at smaller local shops as much as possible. If I'm perfectly honest, I just can't stand big supermarkets. They are so impersonal and I really hate the long queues. There's nothing worse than having to wait in a queue, especially when you're in a hurry. It's such a complete waste of time. I'm also totally disgusted by the way in which larger supermarket chains are taking business away from smaller shops. I'm all for supporting local traders because I think they're incredibly important for the community.

4 Remind students that they should cover all the points on the task card and make use of the time they are given before they speak to make notes of keywords and structure their talk. Point out that the examiner asks the follow-up questions when the candidate has finished talking.

Explain *gadget* and elicit examples before students work in pairs.

Writing 2 p147

Task 1: Maps

Aim
The concluding paragraph of an essay often includes proposals for future developments or further research. Students will need to use conditionals and modals to evaluate the causes, effects, possibilities, advantages and disadvantages of alternative suggestions.

Revise prepositions by eliciting the relative positions of the main features of the map.

For further practice of prepositions, refer students to Photocopiable 9, Exercise 2 (TB page 119).

Refer students to Unit 6, page 96 for revision of conditionals.

1 Students discuss 1–3 in pairs and report back to a small group.

2 Point out that the answers to Exercise 2 highlight the type of language map questions require (prepositions of relative position, result expressions, and language for hypothetical situations and advantages/disadvantages). Tell students that they should not develop any of their points but keep the advantages/disadvantages as factual as possible.

Answers

1 f
2 a
3 c
4 h
5 e
6 g
7 b
8 d

3 Refer students to paragraph structures on Photocopiable 8, Exercise 3 (TB page 118) to decide which is structure being used. Students underline the language for hypothetical situations (*would, if*) and advantages/disadvantages in the answer.

Answers

Structure 2
Para. 1: not attractive/but/easily accessible
Para. 2: easier access/less car pollution/although/congestion
Para. 3: most attractive/however/environmental destruction/pollution/disadvantages

Vocabulary 2 p149

Prefixes

1 Explain the relationship between prefixes and multiples of ten or fractions.

Answers

deca = 10
centi = 100
kilo = 1000
mega = 1,000,000
milli = 1/1000
micro = 1/1,000,000
nano = 1/1,000,000,000

2 When students have completed the matching exercise, point out that fractions end in *-th*.

Answers

1 d
2 e
3 f
4 g
5 b
6 c
7 a

3

Answers

1 centimetre: *one hundredth of a metre (in length)*
centipede: *an insect with many pairs of legs*
2 decade: *period of ten years*
decathlon: *sports event that consists of ten different sports*
3 megabyte: *one million bytes of computer memory*
megalopolis: *a large city*
4 microsecond: *1 millionth of a second*
microclimate: *the weather in a specific small area*
5 milligram: *one millionth of a gram (in weight)*
millionaire: *someone who has more than a million dollars or pounds*
6 nanosecond: *1 billionth of a second*
nanotechnology: *the skill of building very small machines*

Listening 2 p149

Section 4

Aim

By completing summaries and diagrams, students develop their note-taking skills and learn to focus on key ideas.
It is helpful for students to know that lectures are often organized in a similar way to essays: the main point is followed by examples/explanations/opinions/refutations. This section also gives students practice in analysing the organization of a lecture.

1 Ask students to speculate about possible future developments in medicine and industry. As a class, students discuss the probability of these developments.

2 2.17 Students read the questions, then listen and write the answers. The answers are underlined in the recording script below.

Summary completion

Answers

1 computer(s)
2 electronic technology
3 electronics
4 the transistor
5 space
6 energy
7 40
8 supporting

Diagram completion

Answers

9 3–4
10 diseased cell
11 tracking device

Sentence completion

Answers

12 molecular machine
13 could replicate themselves/could replicate

Note: *replicate* is normally a transitive verb (with a direct object), for example *Scientists have replicated the experiment*. It is used intransitively (with a reflexive pronoun) when referring to reproduction and biological processes, for example *The diseased cells replicated themselves* (produced replicas of themselves).

2.17

Good afternoon and welcome to this special seminar on what I believe is one of the most exciting ways in which science and technology have merged, namely through what has become known as *nanotechnology*. While it may be true to say that many inventions in the world of technology have been large-scale, nanotechnology proves that it's possible that what is bigger will not necessarily be best. For nanotechnology involves the science and ability to create something extremely small using computer and electronic technology. If we look back at the past, we see the pocket watch as an example of this. And in its day, this watch was much admired: something small, that could fit into a pocket and yet still function as well as a larger-sized watch or clock. Of course, to find a more recognizable starting point for nanotechnology, we need to look at the world of electronics. Certainly, electronics clearly showed that smaller was better. In fact, the smaller the electronic gadget, the more effective and useful it is. Now those of you who attended my lecture on electronics last week will remember that I spoke about how earlier radio technology was quite awkward and difficult to operate. Then after World War II, the transistor was developed which changed the face of radio. This involved a series of electronic switches that could be placed on a board no bigger than a postage stamp. This meant that an entire electronic circuit could be built in a much smaller area. Naturally, this was not only faster, but it also saved space and more importantly, energy. For those of you who are interested in the transistor, come speak to me afterwards and I'll give you a copy of my handouts from last week.

But moving on with the subject of today's talk, the development of the electronic chip meant that we began to use terms like *microchip* and in doing so place importance on its size being vastly smaller. But as this form of microtechnology developed and literally became smaller, the word *micro* meaning *one millionth*, was replaced with the word *nano* which literally means *one billionth*. There were pessimists who doubted whether a transistor that small would actually work properly, but they were proved wrong and in a modern transistor, what is known as the gate length, or distance the electrons have to travel, is only about 40 nanometres ... um ... I'm sure you will agree, this is unbelievably tiny and not only that, the electrons can travel incredibly fast. And as scientists continue to develop these transistors, there is every chance that they may become even smaller. Of course one of the problems with developments and designs in technology is that they must not only be practical, but also affordable so it might be that companies will not continue supporting nanotechnology, if it turns out to be too expensive to produce in the long-term.

But one area where there has been major improvements is medicine where nanotechnology is being used to fight life-threatening diseases like cancer. Recently, an American university discovered that nanotechnology can be used to help make systems that supply drugs to the body. A quick way to make sure drugs enter the body is by making artificial molecules. These are in the shape of a star and are small enough to go into cells and release the drugs. In this new system, the molecule is made of two star-shapes, connected by a strand of DNA. Each shape is roughly three to four nanometres long. At one end, the star molecule will enter the diseased cell, while at the other end there is a tracking device, which is fluorescent so that it can light up when it has reached a diseased cell. It is hoped that this will be ... um ... a more effective way to fight diseases. But we must not forget that dangers will always exist in the world of technological changes. One I'd like to focus on is as yet unproven and is still the subject of much speculation. It involves the idea that a molecular machine could be built using something called an assembler. This means one machine would make another machine, but of course, these machines would be operated by people. However, some scientists are concerned that there is a real future possibility these machines could replicate themselves and so no longer be controlled by human beings. But while anything in the world of chemistry is probable, I think it's highly unlikely that we could ever develop a machine capable of replicating itself. Still, if anything, it shows that nanoparticles, like any technology, should be carefully and constantly monitored. Next week I will be looking at nanotechnology and recent developments in the field of molecular biology. I hope that you will be able to join me then.

Further practice

For practice in listening for structure refer students to Photocopiable 9, Exercise 3 (TB page 119).

Pronunciation p150

Sentence stress: Weak forms

1 and 2 2.18 In pairs, students repeat these phrases to each other to identify the stressed syllable. Play the recording for students to check their answers.

Answers

(capital letters indicate stressed syllables)

1. it's on the TAble
2. your PHONE is on the TAble
3. your MObile PHONE is on the TAble
4. you HAVEn't LOST your PHONE – its on the TAble

4 and 5 2.19

Answers

(underlining indicates stressed syllables)

1. The bicycle is a great way to get regular exercise and it's much better for the environment.
2. The Internet began as part of the United States military network, but it later began to be used by businesses and academic institutions.
3. Nanotechnology has crept into many areas of our lives.
4. Scientists are concerned that there's a real possibility that these machines could replicate themselves.
5. Next week I'll be looking at nanotechnology and recent developments in the field of molecular biology.

Study skills p151

Understanding question task words

Aim
Question task words are not only used in essay titles, but can also indicate the expectations of a seminar leader and the focus of a discussion.

1

Answers

1 D
2 A
3 H
4 B
5 J
6 F
7 G
8 E
9 I
10 C

Further practice

Refer students to Unit 9 Vocabulary, Exercise 2, page 184 for further practice of identifying question task words.

Dictionary focus p151

Revision of linking devices

Note: Linking devices are explained in detail in Unit 8 Grammar, page 176.

Answers

Sequencing ideas	Expressing conditions	Expressing contrast
firstly, secondly, finally, first of all, next, lastly	if, provided (that), unless	but, although, despite/in spite of, however, on the other hand, nevertheless, whereas/while, yet
Adding further support	**Stating results**	**Expressing similarities**
besides, furthermore, in addition, moreover	thus, as a result of, consequently, so, therefore	likewise, in the same way, similarly
Providing reasons	**Giving examples**	**Concluding statements**
(in order) to, because (of), due to, so as (not) to, so that	for example, for instance, such as	in summary, in conclusion, to conclude, to sum up

10 From me to you

Content overview

Themes

Communication is the main theme of Unit 10. Topics include the mass media, electronic media, newspapers and advertising.

Students will also have the opportunity to discuss controversial topics such as mass communication, freedom of the press and censorship. If students come from countries in which these are politically sensitive areas, classroom debate can be steered towards themes such as individual freedom of expression, privacy for celebrities and the responsibility of the advertising industry for creating markets.

Listening
- two dialogues about using a learning resource centre
- a feedback discussion between a tutor and two students about an essay on the media

Reading
- an academic text about electronic media

Writing
- discursive essays about advertising and the media

Exam related activities

Listening

Section 1	Multiple choice: diagrams Sentence completion
Section 3	Multiple choice Multiple options Table completion Summary completion

Reading

Multiple-choice questions
Summary completion (from a list)
Sentence completion
Yes, No, Not Given

Writing

Task 2	Focus Different question tasks: expecting the unexpected

Speaking Parts 1, 2 and 3

Description
Discussion

Language development

Language focus

Articles

Vocabulary

The media

Skills development

Reading

Identification of main idea and supporting information
Scanning for detail

Writing

Analysing essay questions
Essay organization
Stating your view

Listening

Listening to instructions, suggestions

Speaking

Analysing examination answers

Study skills

Idiomatic expressions

Dictionary focus

Multiple meanings or word forms

Warm up p152

1, 2 and 3 Elicit vocabulary from the whole class to create mind maps for interpersonal and mass communication. Include: *to/a broadcast, transmit/transmission, publish/publication, store/storage.*

Students note their answers before discussing them with a partner.

Suggested answers

1 Interpersonal: *phone, email, letter*
Mass: *book, newspaper, magazine, television, radio*
Either: *computer*
2 Publish: *books, newspapers, magazines*
Transmit and receive electronically: *television, radio, phone, computer*
Store information: *mobile phones, computers*

Reading p152

Identification of main idea and supporting information

The reading passage is lexically and grammatically dense and is intended to challenge students. Remind them that it is an example of a Reading 3 Passage, the most difficult in the exam.

Ask students to predict the contents of the passage from the title. **Note**: It is not possible to determine the purpose of the text from the title. It could be a description, a narrative, a problem / solution or a discussion.

Refer students to Photocopiable 10, Exercises 1–3 (TB page 120). Explain that by scanning the text for keywords, parallel expressions and examples, students will be able to determine the main topics of the passage.

Answers

media: *mass media, new media, mass communication, medium of communication*

communication: *mass communication, private communication, satellite communication, medium of communication, intercommunication, data exchange*

technology/technologies: *computer, communication machine, computerized communication centre, computer based technologies*

cable/satellite/radio transmission: *cable systems, direct broadcasting, telephone networks*

Internet: *interconnected computers, service providers, telecommunication bodies*

1

Answers

1 The first sentence of the paragraph is the topic sentence. The sentence introduces and defines the term *mass media*, which is exemplified and discussed in the remainder of the paragraph.
2 early forms of mass media = *rock paintings, books, pamphlets*

2 and 3

Suggested answers

satellite communication and computer-based technologies including the Internet, personal video recorders, CD-ROMs, compact discs, camcorders, printers, cameras, PCs, cable and radio transmissions, adapted telephone networks

Multiple-choice questions

4

Answers

1 D
2 A
3 C

Summary completion (from a list)

5

Answers

4 mass communication
5 organization
6 country
7 purpose
8 trade

Sentence completion

6

Answers

9 communication revolution
10 storage and retrieval
11 more power/more options
12 transmission

Yes, No, Not Given

7

Answers

13 Yes (in principle, although this isn't happening)
14 No (innovation in technology is limited to a small proportion of the population)
15 Not Given (he comments on the past and the current situation but makes no prediction about the future of the Internet)

Language focus p155

Articles

Refer students to Unit 10 Grammar, page 178 and ask them to complete the consolidation exercise.

Elicit explanations for students' answers by referring to the detailed explanation of the use of articles in sections 1–3 (pages 177–178).

1

Answers

1 c
2 a
3 b

2

Answers

1 f
2 a
3 h
4 d
5 b
6 g
7 e

3 Students discuss their answers in pairs after completing the text. **Note**: If the class is multilingual, it is more productive to place students who speak different languages in pairs, as they will probably have different problems with the use of the article.

Answers

1 a
2 a
3 a
4 the
5 a
6 the
7 a (if there's more than one) / the
8 the
9 [ ]
10 the
11 [ ] / the
12 [ ] / the

Further practice

Refer students to Photocopiable 10, Exercises 4 and 5 (TB page 120) to practise identifying articles and their uses.

Listening 1 p156

Section 1: Multiple-choice: Diagrams

Aim
Students at UK universities are expected to make full use of campus library facilities for private study and research. As a result of the development of electronic resources, most libraries also include learning resource centres, with access to multimedia resources and computers for online research. To study effectively, students will need to inform themselves about a wide range of learning resources and their different uses for academic studies.

1 2.20 Answers are underlined in the recording script below.

Answers

1 B
2 B

Sentence completion

Answers

3 memorize/remember
4 online
5 inter-university
6,7 lectures, seminars (any order)

2.20

[R = Receptionist; S = Student]

R: Good morning. Language Resource Centre. How can I help you?

S: Hi, I've just registered to do a postgraduate degree and I was wondering how I go about joining the Resource Centre.

R: OK, the first thing you need to do is come in and bring some form of identification with you.

S: You mean like my driving licence?

R: Actually, we prefer you to bring in something from your university registration. Students have, in the past, used their passports, but we really do prefer you to bring in your student card with your ID number. This should be on the front of the card and begins with the letters BNP followed by a number.

S: OK, that's no problem. And could you tell me what facilities you offer in the centre?

R: Certainly. We have a range of books, although not as extensive as the library of course. Still you'll find that we do stock some of the books on your reading list, particularly for postgraduate level. The undergraduate students usually find that the main library caters better for their needs.

S: That's good to hear because I was worried about not being able to find the books on the reading list, especially if more than one student wants to use the same book. I find that really frustrating.

R: We are aware of this and it's precisely because of this that we've got a special system whereby you can borrow books, but only on a short-loan basis.

S: And how long is that?

R: There are two types of short-loan books. One is a two-day loan, but the other one is for a single day and must be brought back the next day. We have to be really strict with this kind of loan so there is quite a heavy fine if you don't bring it back.

S: Of course I hope I'm not going to be in that situation, but can you tell me anyway how much it is?

R: Sure, it's £1.75 for a one-day loan and £1.00 for a two-day loan, ... then it's 50 pence a day on top of that.

S: 50 pence for each extra a day!

R: Yes, until you return the book. It sounds steep, but it's really for the students' benefit. You said yourself that it can be annoying not being able to find books you need.

S: OK, fair enough. I presume you also have journals?

R: Oh yes, we have a wide range of academic journals and many of these are available online.

S: Fantastic! Can I access these from outside the college?

R: Yes, you can, but you need to register for this. Er... you can do this when you come in. Basically you need your student ID again and we give you an Internet password, which you can then change if you like. Most students do because it's easier for them to memorize.

S: I'll definitely do that. I'm hopeless at remembering passwords so the only way I can remember one is if I make it up myself.

R: You will also find reading lists online as well as where to find the books so this means you won't have to waste time trying to find books you need.

S: That's really good to know. Knowing exactly where to go to find a book is such a time saver.

R: Mmm ... we also have a special page, which gives you links to other university libraries so if we don't have the book, er ... we can help you get it.

S: Is that any other university library?

R: No, it's just the ones that have joined. It's known as the inter-university library loan system. But you'll find when you go to the web page that quite a few universities have joined and it's growing all the time.

S: What a great idea! I mean, not only to be able to get books, but just to be given the opportunity to exchange ideas with students on other campuses.

R: I quite agree. Oh ... and you'll also see when you come in, that we have a wide selection of videos you can borrow. These range from films to actual lectures and seminars that have been videoed so students have the opportunity to watch them again if they need to or if for some reason, they were not able to attend. And it's pretty much standard that we video visiting lecturers.

S: And are these also available on tape?

R: Yes, they are. And also on CD. Actually, having said that, we don't put all our lectures and seminars on CD, except visiting speakers. Their talks are always put on both so you can choose either.

S: This all sounds fantastic. I never realized there was so much on offer.

R: Yes, we're very proud of our Learning Resource Centre and the university has given extra funding to make sure we can keep all our resources up to date.

Multiple choice

2.21

Answers

8–10 B, E and F (any order)
11 C

2.21

[S = Student; R = Receptionist]

S: I know you mentioned online books and journals ... um ... how many computers does the Resource Centre have?

R: Oh, we have a lot of computers. Basically there are three floors and we have computers on each one, but these are only for searching for the books or articles you may need. They cannot be used for anything else.

S: Oh, I see. So they're really just search engines. And how do you use them?

R: Well, there are a number of ways you can do this. You can use the author's name, but I'm not talking about the first name. Only the surname will work so you can need to know the correct spelling.

S: That sounds quite straightforward. And what are the other ways?

R: Well, you can also do a keyword search, which means typing in a keyword from the title of the book, that's for when you're not sure of the title. But when you do this, you will obviously get a list of books that have this word in the title.

S: In a way, getting a book list like this is really an advantage because it can give you ideas about what other books to read.

R: That's true, but just bear in mind that it takes a little bit longer. Of course, you can also type in a subject keyword and then you'll be given a list of authors and titles around that subject. The final way is, of course, by keying in the name of the book. And, don't forget, there's an information desk so you can always ask someone if you need help.

S: Where is that?

R: You'll find the help desk on the ground floor.

S: Great and are there any other computers to use generally for checking emails and things like that?

R: Yes, there is a computer centre in the basement, but we prefer students to use these computers more for study purposes so please don't spend all your time doing things like checking your emails and you most definitely cannot use it to play computer games. If you are caught doing this, you will be banned from using our computers for two weeks. No, sorry, because of all the problems we had with this last year, this has now been increased to three.

S: One week without a computer would be too much for me!

R: Mmm ... but please don't worry, because when you first come, we'll give you a tour of the library and show you how everything works. Do you know where we are?

Vocabulary p158

The media

Distribute samples of newspapers covering current news items in different ways. Ask students to suggest the audience for which each newspaper is intended and to explain why. Possible audiences are: *young, educated, less educated, right/left-wing, middle of the road, serious, responsible*. Criteria for deciding may include: *size of print, number of pictures per page, complexity of text, objectivity of reporting*.

Brainstorm vocabulary about newspapers. Include: *scandal, gutter press, libel, reporter, columnist, editor, editorial, obituaries, announcements, advertisements, full page, headline, back page, local/national press*.

1

Answers

1 h
2 e
3 j
4 f
5 g
6 c
7 l
8 d
9 a
10 k
11 b
12 m
13 i

2 Students discuss the questions in small groups.

Further practice

Refer students to Unit 10 Vocabulary, page 184 to practise forming nouns from adjectives with words related to the media.

Listening 2 p158

Section 3

1 Students discuss 1 and 2 in pairs before comparing answers in a small group and suggesting reasons for any differences between countries.

2 2.22

Multiple options

Answers

1 C
2 E
3 B

Table completion

Answers

4 bad news
5 broadsheet/tabloid
6 continuity
7 lose interest
8 personality angle
9 comparison

Summary completion

Answers

10 scoops
11 technology/the Internet
12 communicate

2.22

[G = Gabriella; D = Dong; T = Tutor]

G: Thanks for seeing me today. I've been really worried about my media assignment.

D: Yes, me too. I feel much the same way as Gabriella does.

T: Yes, I realized that. Um ... and thanks for sending me your first drafts. I've had a look at them and there are a few things that need revisiting.

D: I guessed you'd probably say that.

T: Right, let's start at the beginning. Um... you both had different problems so I'll speak to each of you in turn. Let's start with you, Gabriella. Tell me, what did you hope to achieve with this assignment?

G: OK, erm ... well I suppose my main idea was really to look at the news.

T: Can you be more specific?

G: Well ... er ... my main focus was really news values, I mean how do presenters and broadcasters, people like that, actually decide what is newsworthy? And as much as I'd have liked to have studied TV news, I had to make the choice between television and newspapers and I chose the latter.

T: Fine. Er ... now that did come across in your introduction. But I wonder if the scope of your essay was too wide? You did try and include an awful lot

G: I was afraid of that. I spent ages reading newspapers and trying to choose the right items. But it's really difficult to know what to include and what to leave out.

T: Well ... shall we look at it together and see if we can make the focus of your essay more specific? Many students find it hard to know what information to select, especially when they read a lot.

G: It would really help me to see where I've gone wrong so I don't repeat this mistake again.

T: OK. Now here in paragraph one, you focus on the negativity in the news.

G: Yes ... um ... I was trying to highlight the fact that really, the general public will usually choose bad news above good. They seem to like it more because bad news sells ... it makes headlines. We like reading about disasters and tragedy.

T: That's true, but I think what you did not explain enough was why this is the case. Is it something in human nature or is it just that this is how we've become accustomed to receiving news? I thought maybe you could have given some examples here, maybe compared two newspapers, a broadsheet and a tabloid perhaps, to look at how they presented a particular negative piece of news. Er ... was it dramatized for example? Which one was more sensationalistic?

G: Ah yes, I can think of so many examples of that. I mean ... you can really see the dramatic effect in an item of news in the pictures that go with the story.

T: Right, now you're getting the idea.

G: Do you think I did the same thing in the second paragraph?

T: Actually, I thought you'd organized this much better. It was clearer. I liked the way you mentioned the value of continuity in the news. Er... continuity is important because quite obviously, the longer an item of news lasts, the more people will buy the newspaper because they are interested in what is happening. Your example of war was a good one because ... er ... most wars last a while so the story will stay in the news.

G: But I also wanted to explain how readers can lose interest in a news story and that was really my main emphasis.

T: Yes, I really liked that part of your paragraph. It showed you'd really thought about what you'd read and had the confidence to add your own ideas. The rest of your essay, apart from a few minor grammar mistakes, was fine.

D: And what about mine?

T: Well, the first few paragraphs were really good: clearly constructed and easy to follow. But er ... I don't think you did this as well in the third paragraph. What you were trying to get across?

D: I was trying to explain about celebrities. What is defined in news terms as the personality angle. The fact that we are ... er ..., you know, interested in stories about famous people.

T: Sure, but I think you need to focus on what this means for the news. Er ... what about looking at how newspapers often publish popular news stories and how this might go against the news attempting to be neutral?

D: So what you are saying is the news is meant to be objective, but actually it isn't really?

T: Certainly. I'm saying you should try and make more comparisons between the objectivity and subjectivity and see which way the news usually tends to go.

D: Mmm ... would you suggest I take a particular news item and compare the way two newspapers report on it?

T: That would be an excellent idea. In fact you could even use some of the ideas from your first paragraph – maybe take a so-called bad news story.

D: That's a good idea and I could use the same newspapers.

T: Yes, but you could also look at two other newspapers with similar styles ... maybe another tabloid and broadsheet.

D: I like that idea.

T: I also felt maybe you could have included the idea of recent news because this links in with what you've already said.

D: I don't quite understand.

T: Well, I'm referring to the idea that newspapers try and get scoops, any big story that has recently happened. You could link this to your first paragraph and even your second.

D: The public is really interested in what is happening now rather than what is old news.

T: And you could bring in the effect of technology on the news at this point. It has affected news reporting and publishing tremendously. If you think about it, the Internet has meant that news can be much more immediate than before so, for example, as something is happening it could be reported and published in a paper.

D: Oh yes, I remember reading once about an earthquake and just before the building collapsed, someone at the top sent an email to a newspaper. I mean this just proves that at the click of a button, we can communicate so much more quickly than before.

T: Yes, that's the kind of thing I'm talking about, but just make sure that you have evidence to support what you say.

Speaking p160

Parts 1, 2 and 3

Remind students that in Part 1 of the exam, although they are not expected to give very long answers, they should try to expand on their answers by giving explanations and examples.

1 2.23 and 2.24 Before listening to the recording, students interview each other briefly by asking and answering the questions in the box about libraries.

Answers are underlined in the recording script below.

Answers

Speaker 1: 1 N (hesitation), 2 N, 3 N, 4 N, 5 N, 6 N, 7 Y (repetition of *popular* and *probably*)

Speaker 2: 1 Y, 2 Y, 3 Y, 4 Y, 5 Y, 6 Y, 7 N

After reviewing the answers with the class, refer students to the recording script on page 207 and play the dialogues again. Students underline the evidence that supports the answers to the questions.

2.23

[E = Examiner; S = Speaker]

E: Do you often use a library?

S 1: Er ... um ... I ... I ... I think I try to use library about ... um ... well ... maybe once or twice a week.

E: OK, and are libraries popular in your country?

S 1: Um ... um ... yes, yes .... libraries are very popular ... yes, they have always been popular in my country.

E: Do you think people will still visit libraries in, say, ten years' time?

S 1: Mmm ... no ... no ... I think this probably won't happen ... um ... I ... I can't say for certain, but I think probably not.

2.24

E: Do you often use a library?

S 2: Oh yes, I using library all the time. [Q3] No one can really live without a library because we needing it for many things ... [Q6] like education and also to broaden our minds. [Q2 and 6]

E: Right. And are libraries popular in your country?

S 2: Oh yes. I can definitely say [Q4] that library is extremely important [Q3] for many people in my country. We have long history of books [Q3] and ... yes, I think, it's true to say [Q4] that people in my country likes reading. [Q3] In fact, they probably very much likes to reading. [Q3]

E: Do you think people will still visit libraries in, say, ten years' time?

S 2: Well, no one can really say what the future holds, [Q2] but I think, yes, we will still go. Even though some people, they say Internet will stopping [Q3] people from reading. But I think there will always be people who prefer the books. [Q3]

2 Before students interview each other in pairs, elicit vocabulary related to each topic, by brainstorming as a whole class. Possible vocabulary for:

Topic 1 (mobile phones): *camera, network, system, SIM card, texting, chatting, ringtones, polyphonic, handset, pay as you go, handsfree.*

Topic 2 (emails): *forward, copy, attachment, signature, insert, accounts, spam, trash, block.*

3 Exercises 3 and 4 are particularly useful if they can be recorded for students to listen to their performance.

Students make notes about both Part 2 topics for one minute each, before selecting a topic at random to interview each other. The interviewer should tick boxes 1–7 (Exercise 1) as they listen to their partner.

4 Students answer the Part 3 questions for each topic and write an additional question, before continuing the interview with their partner.

Writing p162

Task 2: Keeping your focus

Aim

The concepts of *topic* and *task*, which students will need to apply to their analysis of essay titles are discussed in Unit 2. It will help students to understand, in addition, that *focus* is the specific aspect of a topic, the scope of their discussion and *viewpoint* shows their opinion. These components of a title are the criteria by which a lecturer will grade an essay, and students who can analyse their own writing against these criteria are in a position to edit their work more effectively.

1

Answers

1 The first part of the question introduces the TOPIC which tells you what subject you should write about.
2 Following this is the TASK which tells you what kind of essay you should write.

2

Answers

1 D
2 C
3 A
4 B

3 In pairs, students identify the *topic* **(*Tpc*)**, *focus* **(*F*)**, *viewpoint* **(*V*)** and *task* **(*Tsk*)** of the essay title. Review as a class and discuss ideas.

Answers

An increasing number of products for children ***(Tpc)*** *are advertised on TV* ***(F)****. Such advertisements sometimes rely on 'pester power' to persuade parents to buy the products.*

Do you think ***(Tsk: opinion)*** *children's products should not be advertised on television?****(V)*** *Would this be unfair to manufacturers?* ***(V)***

4 Ask students to identify the parts in the extracts on pages 162–163 that relate to each of the elements of the title.

Answers

Student A: topic – *toys*, focus – *not mentioned*, task – *it is my view/I feel*, viewpoint – *not mentioned*
Student B: topic – *advertisements*, focus – *purpose of advertisements (irrelevant)*, task – *a first point to consider/it could be argued (discussion)/I feel (opinion)*, viewpoint – *advertisements are not objective (irrelevant)*

Student C: topic – *children's products*
focus – *TV advertising*
task – *I believe*
viewpoint – *governments control content of advertisements*

Assessment for Student A
Although this extract relates to pestering, the main topic of whether to ban adverts for children's products is not directly addressed at all. The argument that children have too many toys needs to be more directly related to the topic of advertising. As it is, the paragraph does not answer the question. Sentence organization, punctuation and repetition are the main language issues.

Corrected extract for Student A
A further issue is that many children probably already have too many toys. Every year, new products are launched and children learn that by continually pestering their parents they can influence them to buy more toys. It is my view that this can lead to children not being able to enjoy what they already have as they constantly seek new toys. Although it is natural that parents should want their children to have the best things, I feel it is important that they should also try to teach children to value things and to learn patience.

Assessment for Student B
Language is accurate and shows a good range of vocabulary and structures that are well-organized. However, only the final sentence relates directly to the question. The rest is on the general topic of advertising rather than advertising children's products, so the task response mark would be low.

Assessment for Student C
The points are relevant throughout but vocabulary, spelling, grammatical accuracy, range and error density are all poor, so only task response would receive a good mark.

Corrected extract for Student C
A further problem is that if TV advertising of children's products was banned, then how would people (parents/consumers/the public) learn about new things (products)? Such an idea would mean manufacturers could only tell people (parents/consumers/the public) about their things (goods) in magazines, newspapers, or on the radio or Internet. This would not be fair to those companies involved in producing children's toys and clothes. I believe that the answer is not a ban on advertising children's products but for government to have more control over the content of adverts for young people's goods.

5 Students revise each other's paragraphs for *task response, coherence and cohesion, lexical resource* and *grammar*. They underline the parts of their partner's writing that correspond to each of the criteria and discuss omissions or errors.

Different question tasks: expecting the unexpected

6 Students discuss answers to 1 and 2 in pairs.

Answers

1 Tasks = 2, 4, 5
2 (a) general focus: 1, 2, 3, 6
(b) specific focus: 4, 5

For 3, students work in pairs to match tasks 1–6 with task requirements A–F and discuss their answers.

Answers

1 D
2 F
3 B
4 A
5 E
6 C

Stating your view

Aim
In most academic essays, students will be required to take a position on a topic, present their opinion and support it with explanations and examples. Students should be reminded that mentioning opposing opinions and refuting them will strengthen their argument.

7 Students complete the table and check their answers with a partner.

Answers

1 c
2 e
3 a
4 d
5 b
6 f

8 In pairs, students underline the parts of the introduction that reflect the *topic, focus, viewpoint* and *task* of the essay title. They then write their own titles for the essay and discuss them with another pair.

Answers

topic – *privacy of celebrities*
focus – *media coverage*
viewpoint – *different rules for the famous*
task – *opinion*

1 Tougher censorship is required to protect the privacy of celebrities from unwanted media attention. Privacy should be respected whether someone is famous or not. Do you agree or disagree?
2 Opinion essay

9 Students work in groups to complete questions 1–5.

Answers

1 (a) regulation, rule, (protection)
(b) famous people, those who live in the public eye
(c) members of the public, ordinary people, people who are not famous
2 protect (v) – protection (n), privacy (n) – private (adj)
3 censorship, famous, public, publish, raise their profile, monitor, regulations, media scrutiny, negative publicity
4 Yes.
5 Yes.

Point out to students that although this essay is 71 words over the minimum word target of 250, it would not be penalized. Providing an essay remains focused on the question and is well-organized, there is no penalty for going over the word length.

10 Students underline the topic, focus, viewpoint and task in the essay title in pairs, before planning and writing the essay individually.

Students refer to the Unit 10 Model answer, page 196, to identify the main points, supporting points, opinion and refutation in each paragraph and compare these with examples in their own essays.

Study skills p167

Using idiomatic expressions

1

Answers

1 f
2 i
3 g
4 c
5 e
6 h (kept going around in circles)
7 b (are on the same wavelength)
8 d
9 a
10 j

Dictionary focus p167

1 Students find the words in context, check their meanings in the dictionary and add them to their vocabulary bank.

Answers

2 shift (v and n)
3 shift TO/AWAY/FROM, consist OF, potential FOR (n)/TO (v), proportion OF, restriction ON

Grammar key

Unit 1
Tense revision

1

1 decreased
(2 will decrease)
3 will fall
4 is falling
5 was decreasing
6 was falling
7 will be decreasing
8 will be falling
9 has decreased
10 had decreased
11 had fallen
12 will have decreased
13 will have fallen
14 has been falling
15 had been decreasing
16 had been falling

2

1 increased
2 will have doubled
3 has risen/has been rising
4 reveal
5 will level off
6 has been growing
7 declined, has remained stable
8 fell/was falling, began

Unit 2
Sentences and their subjects
Parts of speech 1: Revision

1

1 h
2 i
3 j
4 d
5 g
6 c
7 a
8 e
9 b

2

1 e
2 d
3 a
4 b
5 f
6 c
7 g

Parts of speech 2: Revision

1

1 d
2 a
3 h
4 b
5 f
6 c
7 g
8 e

2

1 d
2 b
3 g
4 f
5 no match
6 a
7 e
8 c
9 h

Unit 3
Compound adjectives

1 There is an increased demand for environmentally-friendly products.
2 Sales of lead-free petrol have soared in recent years.
3 Many doctors still prefer to prescribe sugar-coated tablets for children.
4 Many commuters now travel from London to Paris on high-speed trains.
5 Ready-made foods are a popular choice for working parents.
6 The government was forced to make a face-saving compromise.

Unit 4
Defining and non-defining relative clauses

1 R
2 W: the clause is defining therefore commas should be deleted
3 W: *whom* cannot be used as the pronoun when it is the subject of the clause (and followed by a verb)
4 W: *that* replaces the object *them*
5 R
6 W: must be *who is visiting* or *visiting*
7 W: same problem as 4
8 W: *that* cannot replace *who, whom or which* in a non-defining clause
9 R

Unit 5
The passive

1 are logged
2 cannot easily be replaced
3 can be destroyed
4 is called
5 is created
6 is converted
7 is being altered
8 will be disrupted
9 will be affected

Unit 6
Conditional sentences

1 The city was not chosen as the venue for the Olympics because the public transport system *would* not have been adequate.
2 *Unless* governments invest more money in protecting the environment, future generations will suffer the consequences.
3 *Provided (that)* there are no delays, we should be at our destination by midday tomorrow.
4 If I *won* the lottery, I would be able to travel the world.
5 *If* the government hadn't ignored economic warnings, the country wouldn't be in recession.
6 Edward hasn't *been* offered the job in South America because he doesn't speak Spanish.
7 Before the invention of the airplane, travel to distant parts of the world *would* have been impossible for most people.
8 *Unless* you really want the job, it's best not to apply for it.

Unit 7
that-clauses

no direct object: *admit, announce, argue, assume, claim, *convince (in passive), deny, estimate, insist, point out, recognize*

with direct object: *assure, *convince (active), inform, persuade, remind*

Unit 8
Linking expressions

1 while/whereas
2 for example/for instance
3 While/Although
4 therefore/thus
5 For instance/For example
6 despite
7 Therefore/Thus

Unit 9
Talking about the future

1 will be living
2 will have discovered
3 will have produced
4 will be using
5 will have been replaced
6 will be travelling/will have travelled

Unit 10
Articles

1 the
2 the
3 the
4 the
5 the
6 [ ]
7 a
8 [ ]
9 [ ]

Vocabulary key

Unit 1
Word formation

1

1 astronomical
2 biology
3 biological
4 chemist
5 chemical
6 mathematician
7 mathematical
8 neurology
9 neurological
10 physicist
11 physical
12 psychologist
13 psychological
14 sociology
15 sociological

2

1 astronomy
2 mathematics
3 psychology
4 biology
5 sociology
6 physics

Unit 2
Collocation

1

1 relaxed, healthy, negative attitude
2 disruptive, violent, anti-social behaviour
3 expensive, healthy, stressful lifestyle

Unit 3
Dependent prepositions

1

1 with
2 from
3 in
4 of
5 about
6 of
7 into
8 in

2

1 consume
2 consuming
3 derive
4 derivation
5 renew
6 renewal
7 short
8 short
9 refine
10 refinement
11 detrimental
12 speculate
13 speculative
14 alternate
15 alternative
16 expansion
17 expansive
18 maintenance
19 maintained
20 convenience

Unit 4
Vocabulary

1

1
- 1 d
- 2 f
- 3 h
- 4 b
- 5 a
- 6 g
- 7 c
- 8 e

2 cardiac arrest, dental treatment/care, gastric ulcer/surgeon, nasal accent, optical fibre/illusion, orthopaedic surgeon/shoes, renal failure/disease, auditory information

2

1 reduce/reductive/reduction
relax/relaxing/relaxant/relaxation
stimulate/stimulating/stimulant/stimulation
irritate/irritating/irritant
confuse/confusing/confusion
react/reactive/reaction

2
- 1 having the opposite result to the one intended, to reduce the negative effect of something by doing something that has an opposite effect, to have an effect that is equal and opposite to something else, actions taken to stop something else from happening or having a negative effect
- 2
  - 1 counterproductive
  - 2 counteract
  - 3 counterbalance
  - 4 countermeasures

Unit 5
Weather words: Adjective and noun collocations

weather: *changeable, bright, fair, mild, unseasonable, wintry*

rain: *heavy, light, pouring, scattered, torrential, wintry*

sunshine: *blazing, bright, hazy, wintry*

wind: *gale-force, gusty, light, strong*

snow: *heavy, light, scattered, thick*

cloud: *hazy, low, thick, thunder*

Unit 6

Dependent prepositions

1 of
2 in, on
3 of, of
4 for
5 into
6 for
7 in
8 to
9 in

Unit 7

1 assured
2 denied
3 claimed
4 admitted
5 persuade
6 had already informed
7 announced
8 reminded

Unit 8

Dependent prepositions

1 concern for
2 designed as
3 protect ... from
4 concerned about
5 protect ... against
6 made up
7 designed for
8 supported by
9 support in

Unit 9

1

1
  1 probability
  2 probably
  3 possible
  4 possibly
  5 certainty
  6 certain
  7 likely

2
  1 There's a possibility that a solution to world poverty will be found.
  2 It's almost certain that people will be taking holidays in space by the end of the century.
  3 People who smoke have an increased likelihood of developing heart disease.

2

1 justify
2 summarize
3 analyse
4 discuss

Unit 10

1 society
2 literacy
3 publication
4 efficiency
5 foundation
6 innovation
7 information
8 private
9 traditional
10 adaptation
11 technology
12 numerous
13 (non-) commercial

2

1 conclude
2 design
3 impact
4 principles
5 acquired
6 range
7 primarily
8 distinctly
9 seek
10 computer

Photocopiable pages

1 Learn to succeed

Generating words with prefixes

1 Combine the prefixes in the table with words from the box to make as many new words as possible. Some words can have more than one prefix.

take disciplinary national marital ability belief ordinary estimate direct organize action informed stand act communicate charge cover coloured task sensory nourished

Prefix	Words
dis	
inter	
multi	
extra	
under	
mis	

Parallel expressions and paraphrasing

2

1 Write a one-sentence summary of each of the ten paragraphs in the reading passage, *Battle of Sexes Whirls Above the Science Gap*, Student's Book page 10. Use the parallel expressions, a–i, in Vocabulary, Exercise 1, Student's Book page 12.

1 ______________________________

2 ______________________________

3 ______________________________

4 ______________________________

5 ______________________________

6 ______________________________

7 ______________________________

8 ______________________________

9 ______________________________

10 ______________________________

2 Work with a partner to discuss your answers and check that you have not copied the words from the reading passage.

3 Compare your sentences with the model sentences in the Key on page 122. Underline or highlight any ideas in the model sentences that you have not included in your own summary.

2 Living together

Sentence subjects

1 Look at the following sentences and match all the subjects to their corresponding verbs.

Examples:

<u>The most important thing</u> (subject 1) <u>children</u> (subject 2) **need** (verb 2) from their parents **is** (verb 1) love.

Many <u>parenting strategies</u> (subject 1) <u>that</u> (subject 2) **work*** (verb 2) at one age **stop** (verb 1) working with adolescents.

* *that* is the grammatical subject of the phrase *that work*, while *parenting strategies* is the real subject of the phrase (*<u>parenting strategies</u> work*).

1 Teenagers in England, in particular, but also their counterparts in Scotland and Wales have some of the highest rates of drinking, smoking and drug use.

2 The WHO survey on Health Behaviour in School-aged Children (HBSC) is conducted every four years and interviews 11, 13 and 15-year-olds from the United States, Canada and nearly all Eastern and Western European countries.

3 A third of English, Scottish and Welsh girls rated their health as only fair or poor, with only their peers in Ukraine, Lithuania and Latvia feeling worse off.

4 When the teenagers were asked about quality of life, England was in the bottom half of the league, while Dutch, Swedish and Greek young people were the happiest.

5 Teenagers need to know that exams are not the only measure of success.

Identifying text type and purpose

2 Texts taken from magazines and newspapers are likely to give general information or an opinion about a topic of current interest. They have exciting or controversial titles and pictures to stir the reader's imagination. They often start with a personal story.

Academic texts usually have the purpose of discussing a specific topic in detail. They have informative titles and an abstract, a short summary of the article, at the beginning. They often start with a definition or a point of view.

The following questions will help you analyse the type and purpose of a text.

Type

Does the layout of the text have:
- a picture?
- diagrams or graphs?
- an abstract? (a summary of the content)

Purpose

Does the title or the subtitle:
- include emotive adjectives?
- address the reader directly?
- ask a question?
- state the topic of the text?

Does the first paragraph start with:
- an anecdote? (a personal story)
- a definition?
- an opinion?
- a description?

Does the vocabulary in the first paragraph include words like:
- *suggest, might, evidence, feel, should, seem*
- superlatives
- *X is ...., X is called ...*

3 Look at the layout and first paragraph of the reading passages in Units 1–5 and complete the table below by ticking the boxes that describe the type of publication and purpose of the text.

Type of publication	Unit 1 (p10)	Unit 2 (p29)	Unit 3 (p41)	Unit 4 (pp57 –58)	Unit 4 (p62)	Unit 5 (p73)
newspaper/ magazine						
textbook/ academic journal						

Purpose	Unit 1 (p10)	Unit 2 (p29)	Unit 3 (p41)	Unit 4 (pp57 –58)	Unit 4 (p62)	Unit 5 (p73)
give opinion/ discuss						
inform/ describe						

3 Costing the earth

Describing charts

1 Plan an essay describing and comparing, where relevant, the main features of Diagrams A, B and C.

First, answer these questions about the diagrams.

1 What are the main features of each diagram?
2 What three features are common to all three diagrams?
3 Do the diagrams show changes over time or comparisons at a fixed time?
4 What will you include in the introduction?
5 Will you compare the features by:
   - year?
   - country?
   - % of waste recycled?
6 Will you write separate descriptions of the diagrams or can you make direct comparisons between them?
7 Which feature will you use to link all three diagrams and come to a conclusion?

Refer to Unit 3, Writing Task 1 on Student's Book, page 50; Useful language on Student's Book, page 52 (Making comparisons) and Unit 2, Language Focus on Student's Book, page 31 (Sentence subjects reporting numerical information and comparisons).

2 Write your essay (150 words).

Diagram A

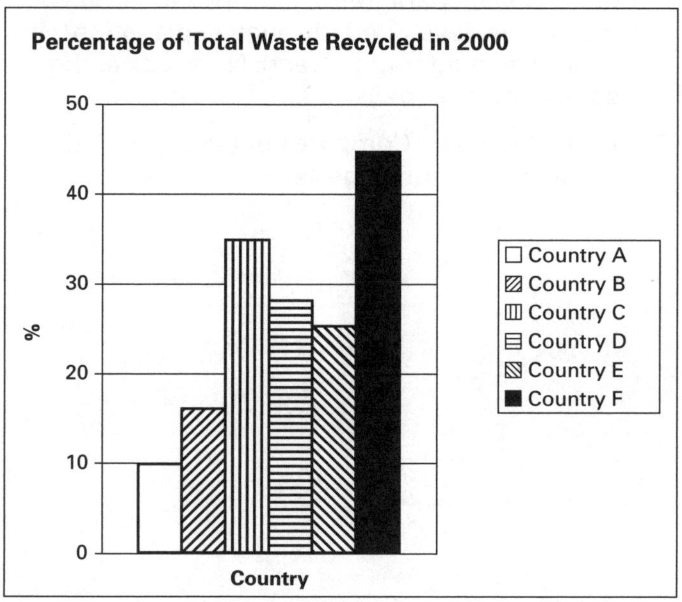

Diagram B

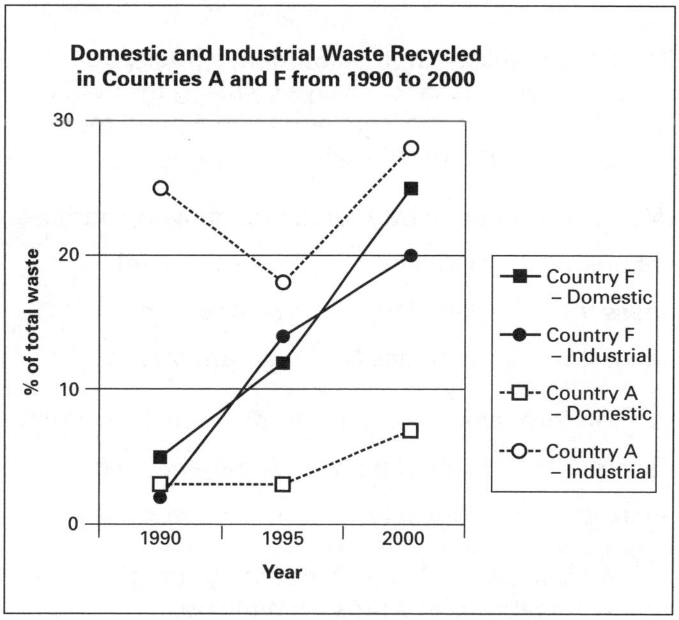

Diagram C

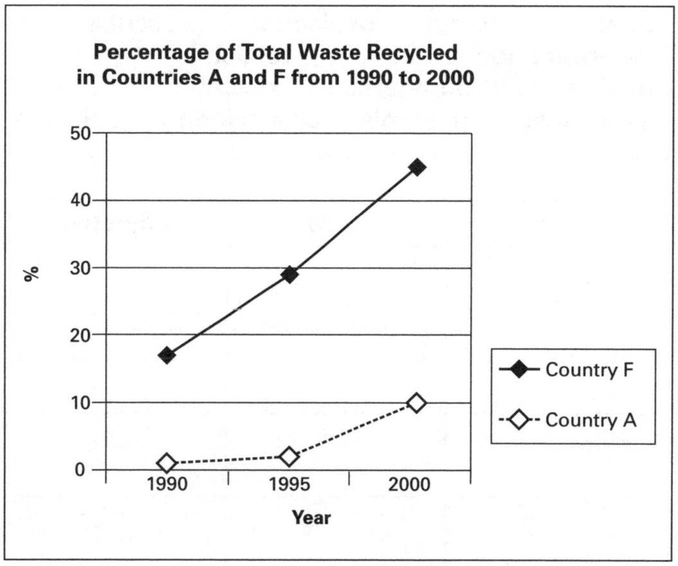

3 Compare your essay with the model answer on page 122.

4 Healthy body, healthy mind

Word study: suffixes

The Study skills section on Student's Book page 71, developed ideas for essays by using the suffix *-al* to form adjectives from nouns on a mind map (*geography – geographical*).

We can form nouns by adding the following suffixes:

-ation (n)	relax (v)	relax*ation* (n)
-ness (n)	kind (adj)	kind*ness* (n)
-ment (n)	increase (v)	incre*ment* (n)

We can form adjectives (and some nouns) by adding:

-ant (adj/n)	stimulate (v)	stimul*ant* (adj/n)
-ive (adj)	digest (v)	digest*ive* (adj)

1 Work in pairs. Using a dictionary, complete the following table with words from the box.

please ill treat confirm
tolerant protect medication prescribe
determination reduced foolish
oxidize discouragement reveal
expensive agreeable appreciation decision

Noun	Verb	Adjective

2 Match the words with the correct suffixes. Some words go with more than one suffix.

1 confirm	-ment
2 ill	-ant
3 tolerant	-tion
4 protect	-ive
5 treat	-sion
6 prescribe	-ation
7 reduced	-ness
8 foolish	-ance
9 oxidize	
10 please	
11 reveal	
12 agree	

3

1 Use the words in Exercise 1 and refer to the structure of an opinion essay on Student's Book page 69 to plan an opinion/argument essay with the following title:

Doctors should be paid for keeping their patients healthy. To what extent to you agree or disagree with this statement?

2 Exchange your plan with a partner and discuss ways you could improve it. When you look at your partner's plan, first underline the main idea for each paragraph, then look at the ways it could be developed (through explanation/example/counter-argument). Now look at the sample plan on page 123.

3 Write the essay. Compare your essay with the model answer on page 123.

5 The world we live in

1 Match the phrases 1–10 with their function in the reading passage *Hurricanes*, Student's Book page 73. Some phrases have the same function.

1 it is called
2 they are formed
3 is made up of
4 it tends to
5 it can last
6 is confidently expected to
7 there does seem to have been
8 on a scale unlikely to be repeated

a speculate
b evaluate
c give an opinion supported by evidence
d define
e describe
f predict

1 ______
2 ______
3 ______
4 ______
5 ______
6 ______
7 ______
8 ______

2 Read texts A–C opposite and underline the words in each text that indicate the writer's purpose (speculate, give a general opinion/personal opinion, describe/define).

A Purpose: ______________________

Life on Earth is sustained by environmental systems which, in their turn, depend on a wide diversity of virgin forest. There are many types of unspoiled forest throughout the world, tropical rainforests, coniferous forests and mangrove swamps being only a few. The weather and the climate depend on the role forests play in the water cycle.

B Purpose: ______________________

Some ecological groups consider that there has been insufficient scientific research on genetically engineered organisms to determine their effect on the environment. These groups believe that science has not yet established how these organisms may damage natural organisms if they are cross-bred and advocates keeping them separate.

C Purpose: ______________________

Poor water quality and the effects of pollution on marine ecosystems and biodiversity are considered to be one of the most serious threats to the sea. It is thought that the establishment of large-scale marine reserves at sea may protect the ocean from some of the effects of land-based contamination and improve water quality both within and outside the reserves.

3 Working alone or with a partner identify the verb (v) and the agent (a) in each sentence. Then rewrite each sentence in the active voice. In two of the sentences you will need to introduce an agent.

Examples:

Passive
Wind is a natural current of air which is caused (v) *by difference in air pressure within the earth's atmosphere.* (a)

Active
Difference in *air pressure* (a) within the earth's atmosphere causes (v) a natural current of air called wind.

1 Certain parts of the earth are heated more than others by the sun, causing air to rise and creating an area of low pressure.

____
____
____
____

2 The sea level is raised by the combination of high winds and low atmospheric pressure.

____
____
____
____

3 Winds that always happen at the same time or in the same way are given names, for example, the Mistral in southern France and the Sirocco in North Africa.

____
____
____
____

4 Wind speed is measured using a rating system called the Beaufort Scale.

____
____
____
____

5 The scale, which was devised by Sir Francis Beaufort, a British admiral, describes wind behaviour at various speeds.

____
____
____
____

4 Use phrases from the box to complete the following description of the process of recycling plastics.

this step involves finally in the following stage the process begins with prior to

[1]____________ sorting.

[2]____________ specially trained workers who separate the plastics manually into different types of polymer and colour.

[3]____________ the plastic may be melted down and poured into moulds to make a new shape or shredded into flakes [4]____________ being transformed into granules.

These are [5]____________ converted into new plastic products.

6 Going places

Signposting language

1 Certain expressions are used to indicate a speaker's intention and guide us through their talk. This is called *signposting*. Some examples of signposting in this lecture about transport (Student's Book page 90) are:

What I'll be doing today ...

My focus will be on ...

Listen to the lecture again (CD 1.28) and make a note of the signposting expressions you hear.

Scanning for proper nouns

2 Highlight or underline all the proper nouns in the reading passage, *The town that tired of life in the shadows*, Student's Book page 91. Classify the nouns in the table below.

People	Places	Organizations	Nationalities	Months

Meaning and context

3 The words in the box below come from the reading text *The town that tired of life in the shadows*, Student's Book page 91. All these words have different meanings in other contexts. Using a dictionary or a thesaurus, complete the sentences with the words from the box.

harness	bounce	remains	direct
conducted	glare	stressed	

1 Although progress has been made in medical research, a cure for AIDS __________ elusive.

2 A multinational company must ensure that its business is __________ according to international laws.

3 An angry person may __________ at another.

4 Before riding a horse, it is important to check that the __________ is firmly fastened.

5 The bank may __________ a cheque if there are insufficient funds in the account to cover the payment.

6 To pronounce English clearly it is helpful to be able to recognize the __________ syllables in a word.

7 When travelling by car, the most __________ route between two cities is usually along a major highway.

7 The world of work

Subject noun phrases

1 Find examples in the reading passage *You Want Any Fruit With That Big Mac?*, Student's Book page 105, of:

1 a subject noun phrase containing: a number, two adjectives and a noun

____

____

2 four subject noun phrases containing a defining clause

____

____

____

____

3 a subject noun phrase containing the name of a variety of apple and a place

____

____

2 Using subject noun phrases, write a short paragraph (80 words) on the following topic:

In the future, all small independent businesses will be eliminated by multinational companies.

____

____

____

____

____

____

____

____

____

____

Underline the subject phrase and circle the main verb in each of your sentences. Compare your paragraph with the model answer on page 124. Underline the subject and verb of each clause in the model paragraph.

Synonyms

3 Refer to the reading passage, *Handling work overload,* Student's Book page 112 and use your thesaurus to find suitable substitutes for the words underlined in 1–5 below. Remember that the alternative word must be appropriate to the context.

1 Non-managers are used to taking <u>orders</u>.

____

2 Sometimes their job allows virtually no <u>discretion</u> ...

____

3 Authority is, on the whole, accepted without <u>question</u>.

____

4 ... they form a link in the chain of command <u>translating</u> corporate <u>vision</u> into reality on the shop floor.

____

____

5 The amount of discretion they are expected to <u>exercise</u> may vary, ...

____

4 Match the words (1–6) with their alternative contexts (a–f). Use your dictionary to help you if necessary.

1 orders	a ophthalmologist
2 discretion	b sports centre
3 question	c international conference
4 translating	d parliamentary debate
5 vision	e confidential information
6 exercise	f catering industry

1 ____
2 ____
3 ____
4 ____
5 ____
6 ____

5 Complete the summary below with the correct figures from the article *Number working past retirement age set to double in 10 years.*

Number working past retirement age set to double in 10 years

The number of people working beyond the state retirement age could more than double within a decade because people cannot afford to retire, according to research.

One in four people between the ages of 55 and 64 feel they cannot stop working at 60 or 65 because they do not have a big enough pension or sufficient savings. A third of women think they will have to work beyond state pension age.

More than a million people are currently working beyond the state pension age, which is 60 for women and 65 for men.

Within five to ten years the Prudential, which commissioned the research, estimates that the number of people working beyond the state retirement age could exceed 2.5 million.

The research shows that 31 per cent of people aged 55–64 who are working full-time, and 38 per cent of those working part-time, do not think that they will retire at the age when they can receive their state pension.

This equates to 1.4 million people. There are a further 118,000 people aged 55–64 who are currently working but who, for financial reasons, are unsure whether they can retire at their state pension age.

Andy Curran, the business development director of Prudential UK said: "Many people approaching the end of their working lives left it too late before they started saving seriously for their retirement, with many feeling they just can't afford to save.

People aged 55–64 who are working full-time save on average only 10 per cent of their salaries with 25 per cent not saving anything at all."

The average age at which people aged between 55 and 64 started saving seriously for their retirement was 33.

Only 23 per cent of this age group started when they were under 30 and 14 per cent did not start saving seriously for their retirement until they were 41 or older.

Mr Curran said: "The choice of retiring at 60 or 65 will no longer be a viable one for a growing number of people."

1 __________ per cent of the population aged between 55 and 64 will have to continue working after state retirement age because they haven't saved enough money for their pension. This includes 2 __________ per cent of working women. At the moment, approximately 3 __________ million people doubt they will be able to retire at 60 or 65.

4 __________ per cent of the 55–64 age group do not save any money. On average, 55–64 year olds began putting money aside for their retirement when they were 5 __________ with 6 __________ per cent starting when they were over 41 and 7 __________ per cent when they were under 30.

8 Art and the city

Discourse markers

1 Complete this introduction to a lecture on famous artists with suitable signposting language.

Good afternoon. [1]______________, could I just check that everyone is at the right lecture. This is the first year Art and Politics module. Right? Good. So [2]______________ a quick overview of the module. [3]______________ we'll be looking at a number of important painters across Europe, and examining the relationship between their art and their politics. [4]______________ I'm going to focus on Salvador Dali. [5]______________ we'll look at the works and politics of Andy Warhol, Lucien Freud, and Pablo Picasso. [6]______________, I'm sure you'll appreciate that lectures can only introduce main arguments and central concepts. I'll expect you to do quite a lot of reading for seminar discussions. Each lecture will take a similar format. [7]______________ I'll analyse a major work by an artist. [8]______________, I'll examine the artist's political views. [9]______________, I'll explain how these views are reflected in their paintings. [10]______________ by comparing and contrasting the ways in which Dali and Picasso expressed their politics in their painting.

2 Match the following discourse markers (1–10) with their functions (a–i). Two discourse markers have the same function.

1 Before we start/To begin with/First things first
2 To start with/I'd like to begin with/I think it'd be a good idea if I give you
3 During/Throughout each week this term
4 In this first lecture
5 In subsequent lectures/In following sessions
6 As time is limited/As we don't have much time
7 Firstly/First of all
8 Secondly/Then
9 Thirdly/After that
10 I'll conclude/I'll bring each lecture to a conclusion/ I'll finish

a establishing the scope of the lecture
b outlining a series of lectures
c giving an overview of the study programme
d dealing with administrative matters before the lecture
e introducing subsequent points
f finishing the lecture
g predicting the content of future lectures
h introducing the first idea of the lecture
i introducing the initial lecture of a series

1 _____ 6 _____
2 _____ 7 _____
3 _____ 8 _____
4 _____ 9 _____
5 _____ 10 _____

Paraphrasing concession and refuting opinions

3 Use both structures in the table to write plans for an essay with the following title:

Art and politics are incompatible.

	Structure 1	**Structure 2**
	Introduction	Introduction
Para. 1	Argument For: point 1 + support	Argument For: point 1 + support Argument Against: point 1 + support
Para. 2	Argument For: point 2 + support	Argument For: point 2 + support Argument Against: point 2 + support
Para. 3	Argument Against: point 1 + support	Argument For: point 3 + support Argument Against: point 3 + support
Para. 4	Argument Against: point 2 + support	Argument For: point 4 + support Argument Against: point 4 + support
	Conclusion	Conclusion

Now compare your plan with the models on pages 124–125.

4 Write one of the essays you planned in Exercise 3. You should write about 250 words.

Compare your essay with the model answer on page 125. Which essay plan from Exercise 3 did the model answer follow?

9 Tomorrow's world

Academic vocabulary

1 Use the academic vocabulary from Exercise 1, Student's Book page 139 and the information in paragraphs 1–4 of the reading passage *Human Population Grows Up,* Student's Book page 138, to write a summary of the history of the calculation of the world's 'human carrying capacity' (80 words).

- Underline the keywords in the reading passage.
- Look for synonyms in the dictionary.
- As you plan your paragraphs, make sure you are using the academic vocabulary in Exercise 1.
- Exchange your paragraphs with a partner.
- Revise each other's writing to make sure you have included key information without copying it from the passage.

Task 1: Maps

2 Look at the drawing of a village and three proposed routes for a new motorway.

Write a description of each of the routes and discuss the effects, advantages and disadvantages of each one. (150 words)

Compare your essay with the model answer on page 125.

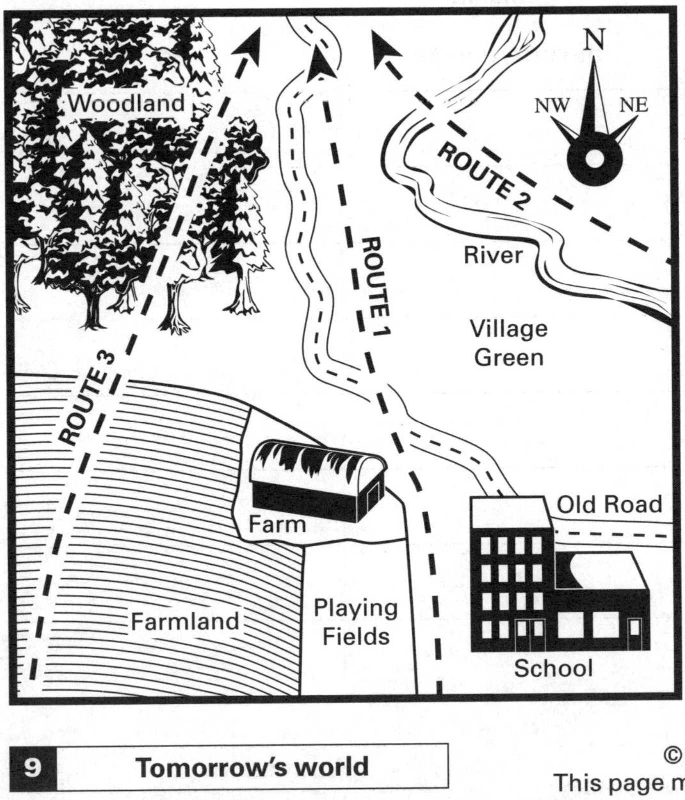

Listening for structure

3 Listen to the lecture on nanotechnology (CD 2.17) again and make notes on the following:

1 main topic ______
2 definition ______
3 example ______
4 topic 2 ______
5 example ______
6 topic 3 ______
7 opinion ______
8 refutation ______
9 problem ______
10 opinion ______
11 topic 4 ______
12 example ______
13 topic 5 ______
14 example ______
15 problem ______
16 refutation ______

10 From me to you

Keywords and parallel expressions

1 Scan the reading passage *New Electronic Media*, Student's Book page 153 and underline the most frequently repeated words.

2 Complete the table with the keywords, synonyms and associated phrases.

Example:
media – *mass communication*

Keyword	Associated phrases
media	mass communication

3 Complete the following summary with words from the essay, Exercise 8, Student's Book page 165. You may need to change the form of some words

The 1__________ of famous people should be 2__________ differently from that of the general 3__________. People who are not accustomed to publicity may suffer as a result of unexpected media attention and should be protected by stricter 4__________ regulations.

The case of 5__________ is different, as they attract 6__________ attention deliberately. In fact, the media has a duty to inform the public about the behaviour of influential figures. The laws governing censorship of the press should be stricter for 7__________ citizens 8__________ with those for public personalities.

Articles

4 Look at the following extract from the reading passage *New Electronic Media*, Student's Book page 153 and highlight or circle the article that refers to each of the words underlined. The first one has been done for you as an example.

> In respect of (the) <u>emergence</u> of any new medium, we can at least recognize the <u>claim</u> of the Internet to be considered as a <u>medium</u> in its own right. This is based on having a distinctive <u>technology</u>, manner of use, range of content and services, and distinct own image. Its recognition as a medium has been held back by the <u>fact</u> that the <u>Internet</u> is not owned, controlled or organized by any single body, but is simply a <u>network</u> of internationally interconnected <u>computers</u> operating according to agreed <u>protocols</u>.

5 Look at Unit 10 Grammar, pages 177–178 and complete the table with the explanations for the use of the articles in the text.

Article (*a*/*an*/*the*/zero article)	Explanation
the emergence	2e

Key to photocopiable exercises

Unit 1, Exercise 1

Prefix	Words
dis	belief ability organize charge coloured
inter	communicate act disciplinary action national
multi	disciplinary national coloured task
extra	disciplinary ordinary marital sensory
under	estimate stand take nourished charge cover
mis	informed direct take

Unit 1, Exercise 2

Suggested answers

A

Lawrence H. Summers apologised for suggesting that women did not perform as well as men in sciences because there were inborn differences between the sexes.

Although there are physical differences between men and women's brains, it has not been established that these affect their behaviour.

B

In the past, women's smaller brain size was given as an explanation of their inability to follow a logical argument.

Men and women use their brains differently, which means it is impossible to make a direct comparison of their ability to think and understand.

C

When they are young, boys and girls perform at the same level as each other, but they diverge during their teenage years.

International research has shown that boys sometimes perform slightly better in math than girls.

Boys' and girls' math performance fluctuated from country to country.

D

Some researchers believe that mathematical ability depends on cultural attitudes to learning.

E

Other researchers believe that women are still treated unfairly in math performance tests.

F

There has been no conclusive evidence that biology does not affect the mathematical performance of men and women.

Unit 2, Exercise 1

1 Teenagers in England (subject 1)
  counterparts in Scotland and Wales (subject 2)
  have (verb 1)
2 The WHO survey on Health Behaviour in School-aged Children (subject 1)
  is conducted (verb 1)
  interviews (verb 2)
3 A third of English, Scottish and Welsh girls (subject 1)
  rated (verb 1)
  their peers in Ukraine, Lithuania and Latvia (subject 2)
  feeling (verb 2)
4 the teenagers (subject 1)
  were asked (verb 1)
  England (subject 2)
  was (verb 2)
  Dutch, Swedish and Greek young people (subject 3)
  were (verb 3)
5 Teenagers (subject 1)
  need (verb 1)
  exams (subject 2)
  are (verb 2)

Unit 2, Exercise 3

Type of publication	Unit 1 (p10)	Unit 2 (p29)	Unit 3 (p41)	Unit 4 (pp57–58)	Unit 4 (p62)	Unit 5 (p73)
newspaper/ magazine	✓	✓	✓		✓	
textbook/ academic journal				✓		✓
Purpose	**Unit 1 (p10)**	**Unit 2 (p29)**	**Unit 3 (p41)**	**Unit 4 (pp57–58)**	**Unit 4 (p62)**	**Unit 5 (p73)**
give opinion/ discuss	✓		✓	✓	✓	
inform/ describe		✓		✓		✓

Unit 3, Exercise 1

1 percentage of waste recycled, domestic and industrial waste, years, country
2 percentage of waste recycled, year, countries A and F
3 B and C show changes over time, A shows a fixed time
4 identify the main features in each graph, highlight the most important trends
5 by percentage of waste recycled
6 B and C by direct comparison, C needs a separate description
7 percentage of waste recycled in country F

Unit 3, Exercise 3

Model answer

Diagrams A, B and C show the percentage of domestic and industrial waste, recycled by six different countries up to 2000. The charts compare international recycling levels in 2000, and illustrate trends in countries A and F between 1990 and 2000.

Diagram A shows that in 2000, the average percentage of waste recycled by the six countries was approximately 25 per cent. Country A recycled only 10 per cent of its waste, while country F registered the highest rate of waste renewal (45%).

In 1990 countries A and F recycled very similar percentages of domestic waste (between 2 and 5 per cent), whilst, at 25 per cent, although country A salvaged a significantly higher percentage of industrial waste (25%). This figure rose in 2000 to approximately 35 per cent in spite of a slump to 28 per cent in 1995. Both countries A and F showed a general upward trend between 1990 and 2000. However, in country A, domestic reuse increased by only 6 per cent, in contrast with country F, where it rose by approximately 20 per cent.

In conclusion we can see that in 2000 international levels of waste recycling ranged between 10 and 45 per cent, with a rising trend between 1990 and 2000 in countries at either end of the scale. (209 words)

Unit 4, Exercise 1

Noun	Verb	Adjective
medication	please	ill
determination	treat	tolerant
discouragement	confirm	foolish
appreciation	protect	expensive
decision	prescribe	agreeable
	oxidize	reduced
	reveal	

Unit 4, Exercise 2

1 confirm > confirmation (n)
2 ill > illness (n)
3 tolerant > tolerance (n)
4 protect > protection (n) > protective (adj)
5 treat > treatment (n)
6 prescribe > prescription (n) > prescriptive (adj)
7 reduced > reduction (n) > reductive (adj)
8 foolish > foolishness (n)
9 oxidize > oxidant (adj) > oxidation (n)
10 please > pleasant (adj)
11 reveal > revelation (n)
12 agree > agreement (n)

Unit 4, Exercise 3, part 2

Model plan

Introduction:

- current situation in UK, no doctor/patient responsibility for disease
- preventative medicine, bonus payments for doctors who offer regular check ups
- discuss advantages and disadvantages of system

Para. 1: encourage check ups to prevent disease, bonus for doctors, example

Para. 2: advantages: incentive for preventative medicine, patient involvement, budget redistributed

Para. 3: disadvantages: expensive, more doctors and nurses, not compulsory, privileged areas

Conclusion: benefits long term, expense – change in government policy, change in attitudes to disease

Unit 4, Exercise 3, part 3

Model answer

Historically, in the UK, doctors have been paid predominantly to cure disease instead of to prevent it. If the government were to introduce a bonus incentive scheme for doctors keeping their patients healthy, medical professionals may take more interest in their patients' lifestyles. This essay will discuss the advantages and disadvantages of such an incentive scheme.

Most people only visit the doctor when they feel very ill. However, a recent report by doctors offering free check ups in the street, showed that many people live with chronic minor ailments. A bonus scheme may encourage doctors to give these patients regular examinations and personal guidance on diet and exercise. Regular check ups for high risk patients, such as smokers, the obese, the elderly and young children, may prevent the development of serious diseases in the future.

The first advantage of offering bonuses to doctors who keep their patients healthy, would be that they would be encouraged to engage in preventative medicine in collaboration with their patients. The well-established system of pre-natal care in Britain is an example of this. Secondly, the health service would be able to save money currently spent on curing serious diseases and invest it in preventative medicine.

The disadvantages of this scheme are, firstly, that it would require more doctors and therefore be more expensive, and secondly that people cannot be forced to attend regular health checks. Additionally, doctors in wealthier areas would benefit more than others.

It is probably fair to conclude that an emphasis on healthy lifestyles would result in reduced expenditure on disease in the long run. However, the social advantages of a bonus scheme for doctors would be long term, and governments may be reluctant to make such a risky investment. However, by adopting such a policy, governments could change attitudes to disease and encourage healthy living. (306 words)

Unit 5, Exercise 1

1 d
2 e
3 e
4 c
5 e
6 f
7 c, b
8 a

Unit 5, Exercise 2

A describe
B give an opinion
C speculate

Unit 5, Exercise 3

1 are heated (v), by the sun (a)
The sun heats some parts of the earth more than others.
2 is raised (v), high winds and low atmospheric pressure (a)
High winds and low atmospheric pressure raise the level of the sea.
3 are given (v), no agent
Meteorologists give winds that happen at the same time or in the same way names.
4 is measured (v), a rating system (a)
A rating system measures wind speed.
5 was devised (v), Sir Francis Beaufort (a)
Sir Francis Beaufort devised a scale.

Unit 5, Exercise 4

1 The process begins with
2 This step involves
3 In the following stage
4 prior to
5 finally

Unit 6, Exercise 1

The first country I'd like to look at ...
... which highlights the point I made earlier ...
Now let's turn to ...
Once again we see ...
Turning now to ...
Next I'd like to look at ...
Finally, I'd like to look at ...
The last country I'm going to mention is ...
To summarize ...
Next week I would like to look at ...

Unit 6, Exercise 2

People	Places	Organizations	Nationalities	Months
Helmar Zangerl	Alps	Bartenbach Light Laboratory	Austrian	November
Manfred Kohler	Austria	University of Innsbruck	Japanese	February
Franz Wurzenrainer	Innsbruck	European Union	–	March
Peter Erhard	Rattenberg	–	–	–
–	Stadtberg	–	–	–
–	Kramsach	–	–	–
–	Australia	–	–	–
–	Canada	–	–	–

Unit 6, Exercise 3

1 remains
2 conducted
3 glare
4 harness
5 bounce
6 stressed
7 direct

Unit 7, Exercise 1

1 50,000, shiny red Gala apples
2 called Apple Dippers, the company that runs the Swedesboro plant, one of six McDonald's apple slicing facilities around the United States, vice-president of the apple association
3 Cameo production in Washington State

Unit 7, Exercise 2

In the future, all small independent businesses will be eliminated by the multinational companies.

In many capital cities throughout the world, the recent spread of multinationals has changed the face of the high street. The traditional mixed bag of small, family owned shops is being replaced by increasing numbers of franchised businesses which follow strict rules about their design and operation. But the changed appearance of our city centres is only a reflection of the more disturbing effects of multinationals. The whole existence of independent businesses is threatened by their inability to compete with large multinationals for supplies, transport or salaries.

Unit 7, Exercise 3

1 orders = *instructions*
2 discretion = *freedom of choice*
3 question = *doubt, reservation, challenge*
4 translating = *converting, transforming, turning, changing*
vision = *ideas, images*
6 exercise = *use*

Unit 7, Exercise 4

1 orders = *catering industry*
2 discretion = *confidential information*
3 question = *parliamentary debate*
4 translating = *international conference*
5 vision = *ophthalmologist*
6 exercise = *sports centre*

Unit 7, Exercise 5

1 25
2 33
3 1.4
4 25
5 33
6 14
7 23

Unit 8, Exercise 1

Suggested answers

1 Before we start/To begin with/First things first
2 to start with/I'd like to begin with/I think it'd be a good idea if I give you
3 During/Throughout each week this term
4 In this first lecture
5 In subsequent lectures/following sessions
6 As time is limited/As we don't have much time
7 Firstly/First of all
8 Secondly/Then
9 Thirdly/After that
10 I'll conclude/I'll bring each lecture to a conclusion/I'll finish

Unit 8, Exercise 2

1 d
2 c
3 b
4 i
5 g
6 a
7 h
8 e
9 e
10 f

Unit 8, Exercise 3

Plan 1

Introduction:

- purpose of art: eternal truth vs social function
- not incompatible, but separable
- demonstrate connection between art and politics, and discuss compatibility

Para. 1: art as a higher truth, for example Michaelangelo's *David*

Para. 2: art as purely visual experience (abstract art)

Para. 3: artists patronised by powerful people

Para. 4: art as propaganda, political statement

Conclusion: art and politics are not incompatible

Plan 2

Introduction:

- purpose of art: eternal truth vs social function
- not incompatible, but separable
- demonstrate connection between art and politics and discuss compatibility

Para. 1: art as eternal truth vs art as political tool (explicit)

Para. 2: art as a subjective, reflective experience vs art as an interpretation of political events

Para. 3: artist free to express himself vs artist as a paid employee

Para. 4: artist as a channel of expression vs artist as a product of his society (implicit)

Conclusion: art and politics are not incompatible

Unit 8, Exercise 4

Model answer

There are schools of thought that believe that the purpose of art is to express eternal truths, and others that it should reflect political ideas or the artist's response to current events. As great art throughout history has served both purposes, it is not possible to say that art and politics are incompatible. They can, however, be detached from each other. This essay will discuss the relationship between art and politics.

Art is generally divorced from political aims when its purpose is to express an abstract ideal, like beauty or suffering. This is typical of classical art, which appeals to the higher senses. An example of this would be the famous statue of Michaelangelo's *David*.

Another case in which there is no direct connection between art and politics is that of abstract art, the sole aim of which is predominantly to create a sensory impression of colour and shape.

On the other hand it could be argued that no art can be detached from its environment. In the past, when they were financed directly by powerful people, artists were obliged to reflect the politics and interests of their wealthy patrons. For example, Leonardo Da Vinci's designs served the military interests of his financial supporters.

Art can also be more specifically associated with politics in the form of propaganda and cartoons. Examples of art serving politics are found throughout the world, from the British posters of the First World War to those of the Cultural Revolution in China.

To summarize, although some forms of art can be detached from politics more easily than others, art and politics are far from incompatible. On the contrary, art and politics are, in many cases, closely associated, with art often responding to the needs and pressures of political events. (294 words)

The essay follows Plan 1.

Unit 9, Exercise 1

Concerns about the sustainability of human society have been repeated throughout history, from 1600 BC to the present day. Seventeenth-century estimates stood at approximately 13 billion, while recently it was calculated that the world could feed and shelter a population half as large again as the current one. Estimates have been based on calculations of population density and on the area of land available for cultivation. It has recently been determined that the population is consuming global resources faster than they can be replaced. (85 words)

Unit 9, Exercise 2

The plan shows three possible routes for a new motorway. Each of the routes runs through or near a village and has distinct advantages and disadvantages.

Route 1 crosses the village from south to north between the school building and the playing fields, whilst Route 2 crosses over the river to the north of the village. An alternative route, Route 3, runs from the south of the village across the farmland and through the woods. Routes 2 and 3 do not pass directly through the village centre, whereas Route 1 divides the school from the playing fields and cuts the village in two. Route 2, on the other hand, requires an expensive bridge over the river and Route 3 reduces the amount of farmland, affecting local labour and the farmer's income. The advantage of Route 1 is that it follows the existing road.

All three routes represent a disruption to village life, but although Route 2 may be more expensive to build, its overriding advantage is that it does not pass through the centre of the village. (179 words)

Unit 9, Exercise 3

Answers are in italics in recording script below.

Good afternoon and welcome to this special seminar on what I believe is one of the most exciting ways in which science and technology have merged, namely through what has become known as *nanotechnology*. While it may be true to say that many inventions in the world of technology have been large-scale, nanotechnology proves that it's possible that what is bigger will not necessarily be best. For nanotechnology involves *the science and ability to create something extremely small using computer and electronic technology*. If we look back at the past, we see *the pocket watch* as an example of this. And in its day, this watch was much admired: something small, that could fit into a pocket and yet still function as well as a larger-sized watch or clock. Of course, to find a more recognizable starting point for nanotechnology, we need to look at the world of *electronics*. Certainly, electronics clearly showed that smaller was better. In fact, the smaller the electronic gadget, the more effective and useful it is. Now those of you who attended my lecture on electronics last week will remember that I spoke about how earlier radio technology was quite awkward and difficult to operate. Then after World War II, the *transistor* was developed which changed the face of radio. This involved a series of electronic switches that could be placed on a board no bigger than a postage stamp. This meant that an entire electronic circuit could be built in a much smaller area. Naturally, this was not only faster, but it also saved space and more importantly, energy. For those of you who are interested in the transistor, come speak to me afterwards and I'll give you a copy of my handouts from last week.

But moving on with the subject of today's talk, the development of the *electronic chip* meant that we began to use terms like *microchip* and in so doing place importance on its size being vastly smaller. But as this form of microtechnology developed and literally became smaller, the word *micro* meaning *one millionth*, was replaced with word *nano* which literally means *one billionth.* There were *pessimists who doubted whether a transistor that small would actually work* properly, *but they were proved wrong* and in a modern transistor, what is known as the gate length, or distance the electrons have to travel is only about 40 nanometres ... um ... I'm sure you will agree, this is unbelievably tiny and not only that, the electrons can travel incredibly fast. And as scientists continue to develop these transistors, there is every chance that they may become even smaller. Of course one of the problems with developments and designs in technology is that they must not only be practical, but also affordable so it might be that *companies will not continue supporting nanotechnology, if it turns out to be too expensive* to produce in the long-term. Having said that, today parts of jet engines, car engines and even cameras are now designed using nanotechnology which shows how, without us maybe realizing it, *this form of technology has crept into many areas of our lives. I'm certain that in specific areas, this will still be the order of the day* and we only have to look at how cameras keep getting smaller to see how this could be the shape of cameras to come.

But one area where there has been major improvements is *medicine* where nanotechnology is being used to fight life-threatening diseases like cancer. Recently, an American university discovered that nanotechnology can be used to help make systems that supply drugs to the body. A quick way to make sure drugs enter the body is by making *artificial molecules.* These are in the shape of a star and are small enough to go into cells and release the drugs. In this new system, the molecule is made of two star-shapes, connected by a strand of DNA. Each shape is roughly three to four nanometres long. At one end, the star molecule will enter the diseased cell, while at the other end there is a tracking device, which is fluorescent so that it can light up when it has reached a diseased cell. It is hoped that this will be ... er ... a more effective way to fight diseases. But we must not forget that *dangers* will always exist in the world of technological changes. One I'd like to focus on is as yet unproven and is still the subject of much speculation. It involves the idea that a *molecular machine* could be built using something called an *assembler.* This means one machine would make another machine, but of course, these machines would be operated by people. However, some scientists are concerned that there is a real future possibility these *machines could replicate themselves* and so no longer be controlled by human beings. But while anything in the world of chemistry is probable, *I think it's highly unlikely* that we could ever develop a machine capable of replicating itself. Still, if anything, it shows that nanoparticles, like any technology, should be carefully and constantly monitored. Next week I will be looking at nanotechnology and recent developments in the field of molecular biology. I hope that you will be able to join me then.

Unit 10 Exercise 1

media
communication
computer
technology
transmission
new

Unit 10 Exercise 2

media	medium, mass communication
communication	communication technologies, communication revolutions satellite communication, transmission, intercommunication data exchange
computer	communication machine, network, interconnected computers, service providers
technology	video recorders, CD-ROM, compact disc, remote control device, camcorders, PCs, printers, cameras
transmission	cable, satellite, radio
new	innovations

Unit 10, Exercise 3

1 privacy
2 protected
3 public
4 censorship
5 celebrities
6 media
7 ordinary
8 compared

Unit 10, Exercise 4

the claim
a medium
a (distinctive) technology
the fact
the Internet
a network
computers (no article)
protocols (no article)

Unit 10, Exercise 5

Article (*a/an/the/*zero article)	**Explanation**
the emergence	2e
the claim	2e
a medium	1d
a (distinctive) technology	1c
the fact	2e
the Internet	2a
a network	1b
computers	3
protocols	3